Gandydancer's Children

Frank Wendell Call

Gandydancer's Children

A RAILROAD MEMOIR

University of Nevada Press ▲▲ Reno & Las Vegas

University of Nevada Press, Reno, Nevada 89557

Manufactured in the United States of America
Design by Carrie House

All illustrative material in this book is the property of the family of Frank Wendell Call, unless otherwise specified.

Map by Cameron Sutherland

Library of Congress Cataloging-in-Publication Data
Call, Frank Wendell, b. 1920.
Gandydancer's children : a railroad memoir / Frank Wendell Call.
p. cm.
Includes bibliographical references.
ISBN 0-87417-353-1 (alk. paper)
1. Call, Frank Wendell, b. 1920. 2. Call family.
3. Railroad construction workers—Nevada—Biography.
4. Nevada—Social life and customs. I. Title.
HD8039.R3152 U63 2000
385'092—dc21 00-008543

The paper used in this book meets the requirements of American National Standard for Information Sciences—Permanence of Paper for Printed Library Materials, ANSI Z39.48-1984. Binding materials were selected for strength and durability.

Frontispiece: Frank Wendell Call, Montello, Nevada, 1939.

ISBN-13: 978-0-87417-353-6 (pbk. : alk. paper)

Contents

Illustrations

Preface

In November 1928, Frank E. Call, a salesman, moved his family from a large, comfortable home in the city to a tiny two-room shanty in an isolated railroad way station in northeastern Nevada. He was to work as a "gandydancer," a track laborer on the railroad. He planned to become a section foreman.

Section foremen were well-off. They ate well and dressed well, and most of them were able to buy a new car every year or two. After six months' experience as a track laborer, Frank planned to take an examination that would qualify him as a section foreman and then start bidding on foreman jobs as they became available—a process that he estimated would take about a year and a half to two years. The first part of his plan worked very well. In six months he qualified and became relief foreman on the Salt Lake Division of the Southern Pacific.

However, the stock market crash in October 1929 and the Great Depression that followed upset his timetable. The rich farms and orchards in California began shipping less and less fruit as the money in Chicago and New York dried up. The railroad, to stay in business, began eliminating sections and section foremen's jobs. With each cut, Frank was dropped another notch down the seniority list. Consequently, he spent the next ten years as a gandydancer with frequent assignments as relief foreman.

Meanwhile, his six children adapted to living alongside the railroad tracks in a succession of primitive houses without electricity or indoor plumbing. They went to one-room schools. They roamed the surrounding mountains and deserts. They played with railroad torpedoes and fusees. They swam in the perilous Humboldt River. They explored old mine tunnels. They thought they were the luckiest kids in the world. This is their story.

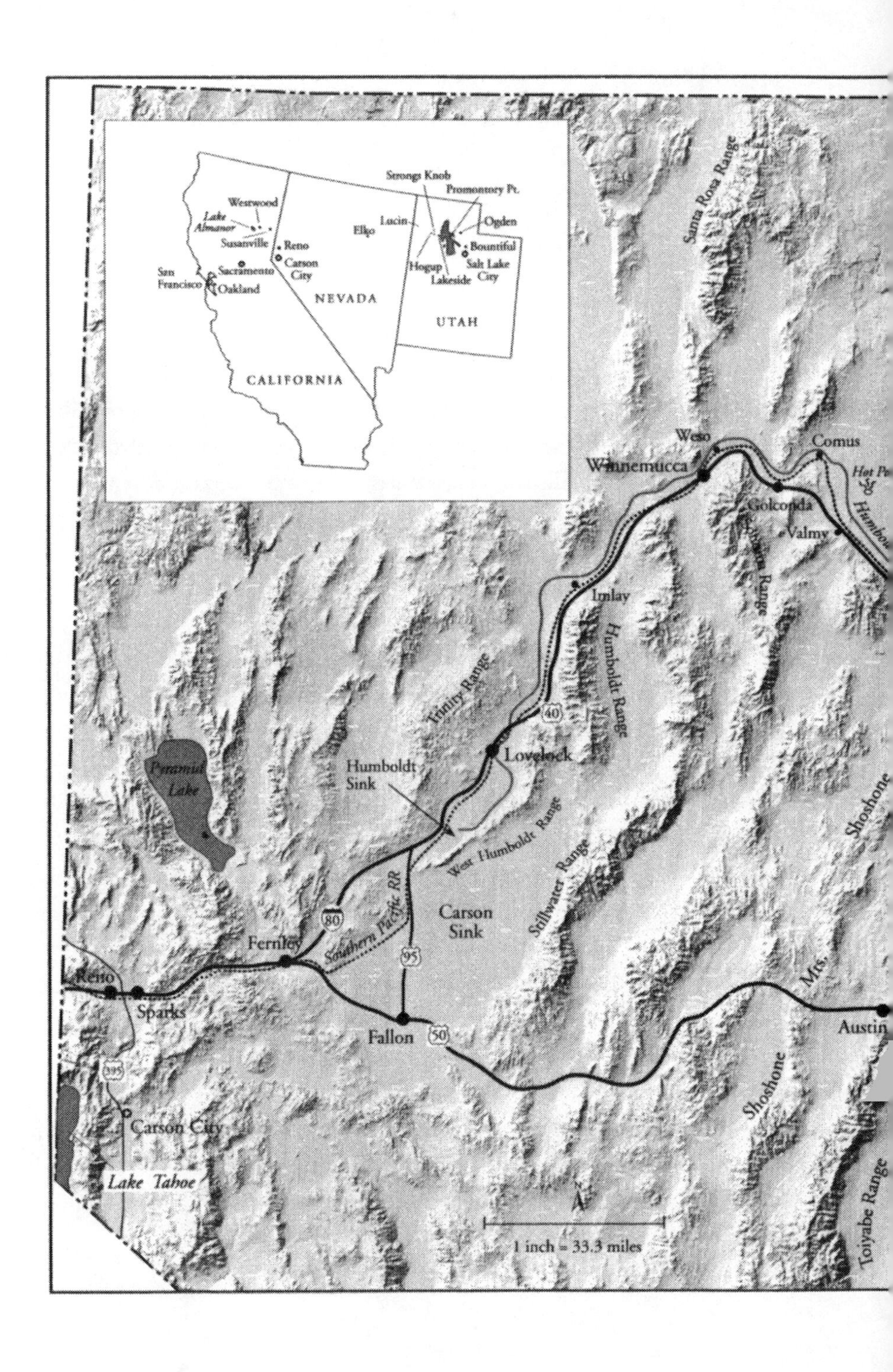
Strongs Knob
Promontory Pt.
Westwood
Lake Almanor
Ogden
Lucin
Elko
Susanville
Reno
Bountiful
Carson City
Hogup
Salt Lake City
Lakeside
San Francisco
Sacramento
Oakland
NEVADA
UTAH
CALIFORNIA
Santa Rosa Range
Weso
Comus
Winnemucca
Golconda
Valmy
Imlay
Humboldt Range
Trinity Range
Lovelock
Pyramid Lake
Humboldt Sink
West Humboldt Range
Stillwater Range
Shoshone
Carson Sink
Southern Pacific RR
Fernley
Reno
Sparks
Fallon
Austin
Mts.
Shoshone
Carson City
Lake Tahoe
Toiyabe Range
1 inch = 33.3 miles
40
80
95
50
395

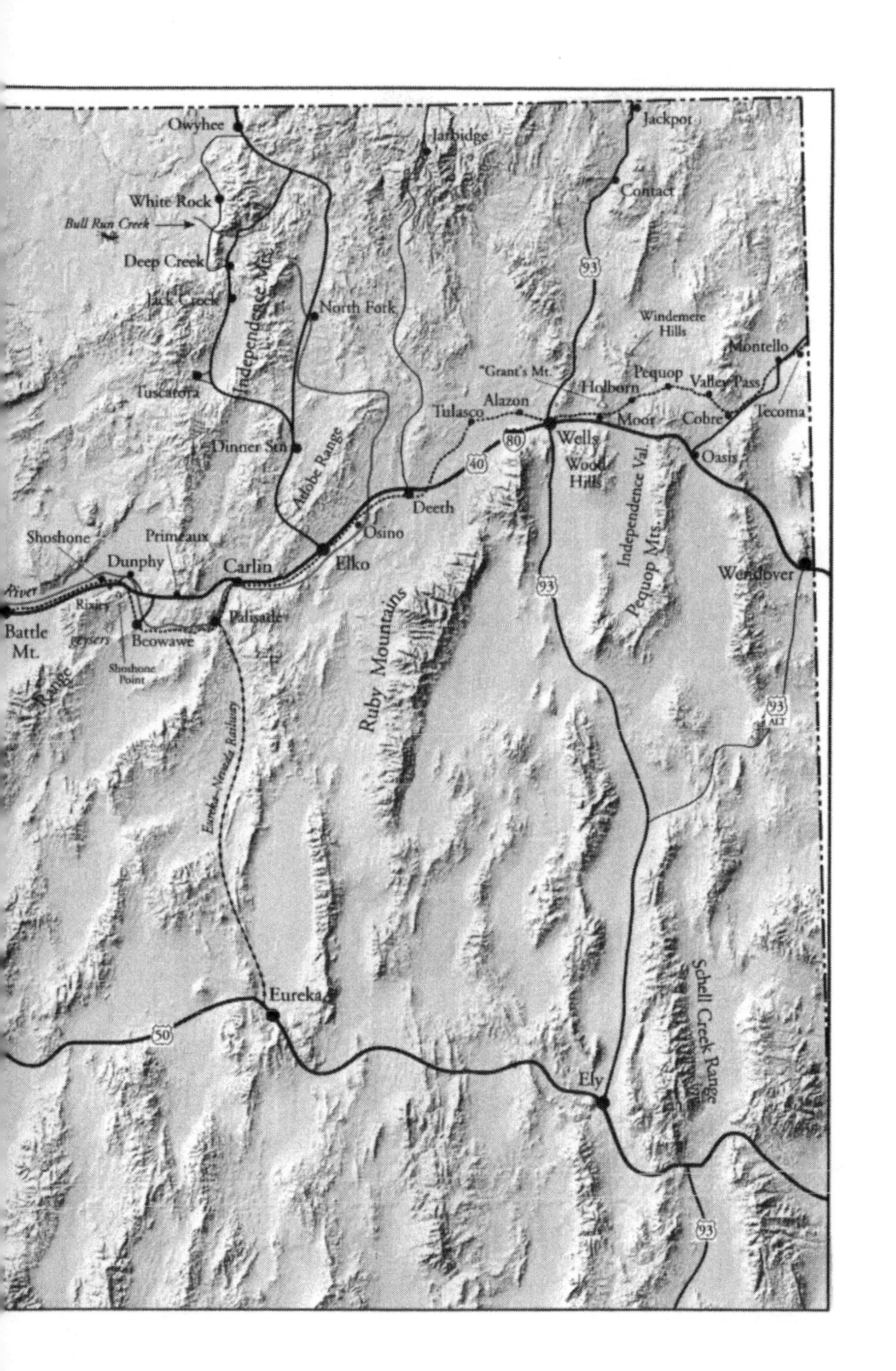
Owyhee
Jarbidge
Jackpot
Contact
White Rock
Bull Run Creek
Deep Creek
Jack Creek
Independence Mt.
North Fork
Tuscarora
Windemere Hills
Montello
"Grant's Mt.
Holborn
Pequop
Valley Pass
Tecoma
Tulasco
Alazon
Moor
Cobre
Wells
Oasis
Dinner Stn.
Adobe Range
Wood Hills
Independence Val.
Pequop Mts.
Deeth
Osino
Elko
Shoshone
Primeaux
Dunphy
Carlin
Wendover
River
Battle Mt.
geysers
Beowawe
Palisade
Shoshone Point
Range
Ruby Mountains
Eureka-Nevada Railway
Eureka
Ely
Schell Creek Range
93
80
40
50
93 ALT

Gandydancer's Children

I

Moor

It must have been in August or September that Dad brought home the news that changed our life from humdrum existence in the city to high adventure in the Nevada desert.

"I'm going to work on the railroad," he said. "We're moving to Nevada, to a little place called Moor. There's a small forest of trees there, and I think we will all like it."

Mother's eyes sparkled with delight. "A real forest!" she exclaimed. "Won't that be grand!"

Mother, who had grown up near the green forests of Denmark, had often described to us the joy she had taken in wandering through their cool depths in search of berries or forget-me-nots. Although she loved her adopted land, Utah's dry climate was far different from the green lushness in which she had spent her childhood. A forest, even if it was a small one, would certainly remind her of far-off Jutland.

"What's a forest?" four-year-old Dale wanted to know.

"It's a place with trees, like down at the park, but it doesn't have cement walks through it," volunteered Rey, who was six and thought he knew everything.

I thought Rey had come fairly close, but I wasn't sure what a real forest would be like. There were no forests near Ogden. Oh, we had seen pictures. And we knew from Mother's tales, such as "Hansel and Gretel," that a forest was a place where you could easily get lost. So we older children began to look forward to the "small forest" with shivery anticipation.

There were eight of us in the Frank Elwood Call family in that year, 1928. At eight, I was the oldest of the six children. Besides Rey and Dale, there was Grant, who was five; my only sister, Adona, who was two; and baby brother Cyril, who had been born in January of that year.

We spent the next few weeks busily preparing for our big move. We were surprised to learn that, except for our clothes, nearly everything we owned in our big old house, including the furniture, had to go into storage.

"We will be living in a small house for a while," Dad explained. "There just won't be room for much." Even my treasured bike had to remain behind. "There's no place out there to ride it," he said.

Living in Nevada was going to be a new experience for us all.

Although Dad had met Mother while he was a stationary fireman[1] at the School for the Deaf and Blind in Ogden, Utah—she worked in the laundry at the school—he had been a salesman most of his adult life. He had been selling brooms in Butte, Montana, when I was born, and he had been selling life insurance in Ogden when most of my brothers and my sister were born.

During most of 1928, Dad had been working for the L. H. Manning Company, which operated a series of commissaries along the Southern Pacific Railroad's Salt Lake Division in places too small and too isolated to have a store. The day-to-day operation of each commissary was handled by the section foreman. It was Dad's job to maintain the commissaries' stocks, supervise their operation, and collect receipts from the foremen.

With his frequent trips to Nevada, Dad noticed that the section foremen were well-off. They received a good salary, with house, lights, and fuel thrown in. They ate well and dressed well, and most of them were able to buy a new car every year or two. Dad's plan was to work as a track laborer, a "gandydancer," for six months,[2] take the test to qualify as a section foreman, then spend the next year or year and a half as a relief foreman, until he had enough seniority to "bid" a job as a permanent section foreman.

Our big move came in November. I don't remember how we got ourselves and our baggage to the station. I do remember sitting on a bench in the bustling Ogden Union Station waiting for our train.

"What are we sitting here for?" Rey wanted to know. "Why don't we get on the train?"

"Just be patient," Dad replied. "The train is in the yard, but we can't get on until it is called. When you hear the stationmaster call Train Number 27, then we can go."

Finally, the stationmaster got around to calling our train. He took his time about it, singing out two or three words at a time as his voice echoed throughout the cavernous waiting room.

"Southern Pacific . . . Overland Limited . . . Train Number 27 . . . westbound . . . for . . . Elko . . . Winnemucca . . . Reno . . . Sacramento . . . Oakland . . . San Francisco . . . now ready on Track Eight. All abo-o-o-o-ard!"

By the time he got to the "all aboard" part of his announcement, there were hardly any passengers left in the waiting room. We were all moving through the doors marked TO TRAINS and down the steps to the tunnel under the tracks. To me it seemed we had to walk a long way in that tunnel to get to Track 8.[3] Then we had to go up some steps and walk along the train until we got to the car in which we were to ride.

There were no seat reservations. We found seats in one of the day coaches and waited for the train to start. This turned out to be an impatient time for me. Then and later, once I got on a train, I was always anxious for it to get moving. I was never really happy on a train unless it was rolling at full speed.

Eventually, a trainman shouted, "'bo-o-a-rd!" and the train indeed started moving, but so gradually that at first I wasn't sure it was. However, it rapidly picked up speed, and soon we were out of the city, rolling alongside the Weber River, heading toward the Great Salt Lake.

That first time crossing the lake by train was exciting. The "news butcher,"[4] who had set up his display across two facing seats at the head of our car, gave a little speech about "going to sea by rail." He offered for sale colored postcards with little bags of salt attached. The postcard had a picture of a passenger train crossing the lake on the trestle. If I had had any money I would have bought one.

"It's just as well," Dad said. "It's a waste of money. I'm not convinced the salt in that little bag came from the Great Salt Lake anyway." He had a low opinion of news butchers. I, on the other hand, was fascinated by the display. Across the train windows above and between his facing seats he had strung a cord holding several brightly colored pillowcases that looked like they were made of silk. They depicted scenes from various spots along the way, such as Lake Tahoe. Stacked on the seats was an attractive display of candy bars, magazines, postcards, books, and other items he hoped to sell. The item I liked the best was a glass locomotive filled with tiny, brightly colored candies. How I wanted one of those! But, of course I didn't have the money.

As we crossed the lake, the sky was overcast and the wind was blowing from the south, churning up foam among the pilings that supported the wooden trestle. Long, white streamers of foam floated on the water to the north of the trestle. The trip across the twelve miles of trestle took about forty minutes because of a permanent "slow order" prohibiting the train from going faster than twenty miles an hour. In the years to come, crossing the Great Salt Lake would become for me the most monotonous part of the journey to and from Nevada, but this first time it was great fun.

The trip to Moor took about five hours, with brief stops at places with fascinating names: Promontory Point, Lakeside, Lucin, Montello, Cobre, Pequop. At every stop, a few people would get off. Much too soon for me, it was our turn. The train slowed and came to a stop. We climbed down from the train to a dirt platform just east of an old boxcar that served as the depot. A sign on the end proclaimed that this was Moor. Yet I was not ready to get off. Someday, I thought, I am going to get back on this train and ride it all the way to the Pacific Ocean.

I remember our family walking west along the track from the little station house. The train was still standing as we picked up our boxes and bundles and started the short walk through a small cut to our new home.[5] Rey and I—eager to see what was at the other end of the cut—were walking well in front of the rest of the family.

We walked along, staring in awe at the huge driving wheels and side rods of the 4300 series engine, so close we could have reached out and touched them if we had dared.[6] The monster engine seemed to be alive. The fire roared in the firebox, and wisps of steam curled from mysterious places. Just as we approached the front of the engine, a jet of steam blasted out of a little nozzle in front of us. I was so startled, yet I was frozen where I stood. What I wanted to do was drop the bundle I was carrying and scramble up the side of the cut and run as far away from that monster as possible, but I couldn't get my feet to move. I looked up over my shoulder at the engineer high up in the cab, who grinned and waved—big joke! He then did some mysterious things inside the cab, and the train smoothly, but with a lot of chuffing and clanking, began to move ahead of us. Each car that went past was moving faster than the one before. In less than a minute the train was gone out of sight around a curve. That was my introduction to the steam locomotive. Ever since that day, I have had a slightly nervous feeling whenever I walked alongside one of those "hogs" when it was fired up—especially when some clown was up in the cab.[7]

"But where's the forest?" Dale demanded, looking around.

"You'll see it just as soon as we get out of this cut," Dad promised. The sides of the cut lowered steadily as we walked, and suddenly there was our forest. But what a strange-looking forest! Instead of the tall trees I had imagined, with shaded aisles between stately trunks and a leafy canopy high overhead, there were stunted juniper and piñon trees perhaps only twice Dad's height—and Dad was a short man, just a little over five feet tall. They looked like a display of Christmas trees filling the valley and growing right up to the tops of the low mountains to the north and south.

"And there's our new home," Dad said, as we emerged from the cut.

We stopped and stared in disbelief.

2

The Tie House

It wasn't much of a house. Built of railroad ties, and with a dirt roof, it squatted brown and ugly in the snow. From the outside, it looked more like a chicken coop than a place for people to live—and it didn't look much better when we got inside. There were just two rooms, each perhaps twelve feet square. There was a connecting door, and each room had a door to the outside. The west room had a closet and a potbellied heating stove. The east room had a place for a range and a shelf big enough to hold a water bucket and a dishpan. It now became clear why we had stored the furniture from our rambling eight-room house in Ogden.

"But where's the bathroom?" Grant wanted to know. In spite of being only five, he was a practical sort. He didn't have to go just then, but he thought it would be good to know where the facility was when the time came.

"It's right there," Dad replied, pointing through the window in the north wall of the east room. We crowded around to look, and there on the other side of a snowdrift stood our first outdoor privy.

There was no running water in the house. All the water used for drinking, cooking, washing, and bathing had to be carried in buckets from the cistern across the tracks. Hot water had to be heated on the stove. There wasn't even a sink or a drain; used water was simply thrown out the door. And of course there was no electricity. If Mother was disappointed, she never showed it. The first thing she did after she took off her hat was to send out for water.

"Come along, boys," Dad said to Rey and me. "It will be your job to bring in all the water your mother needs."

Taking up two buckets, he led us across the tracks to the cistern and showed us how to work the pump. He carried the two buckets back to the house and then declared, "From now on, it's all yours!"

A full three-gallon pail of water weighs about twenty-five pounds. I could carry a full bucket home only with great difficulty, and then only with frequent stops along the way to rest. When I was sent for a bucket of water, a half bucket was what I usually brought, which meant that I had to go right back and get at least another half bucket. The trip back across two sets of main line tracks and across the yard carrying a half bucket of water seemed like such a long way, and Mother always seemed to need such a great deal of water, especially on bath night.

Saturday night, of course, was bath night. To save water, Mother devised her own system for bathing six children in the same water and getting them all clean. All bathing was done in a No. 3 galvanized washtub placed close to the stove. She heated the water on the stove in a wash boiler, one of those oblong containers that fit across two stove lids. If the lids were removed from under the boiler, the water heated faster with less fuel, but the burners blackened the bottom of the boiler with soot. Rey and I were the water carriers, and we had to carry enough water home to fill the wash boiler. It took us several trips. When the water was hot enough, it was dipped from the boiler into the washtub to a level about one-fourth full.

The first one into the tub rinsed himself off, washed with soap, rinsed again, and got out. The second one into the tub did the same, except that when the second rinse was finished, he stood up, and Mother gave him another rinse with warm, fresh water from the wash boiler. Bathing usually proceeded from the oldest and biggest down to the smallest. The smaller the child, the less displacement took place in the tub, leaving more room for all that fresh rinse water.

It seemed to Rey and me that we were always carrying water. There was a never-ending need for water that continually interrupted whatever fascinating thing we happened to be doing. In later years, Mother insisted that she herself carried more water from the cistern than the two of us put together, and Dad probably carried an equal amount. Maybe so. We weren't always handy to fetch water, and after all, they carried full buckets—and usually two at a time!

The one luxury we had brought with us from our home in Ogden was the kitchen range. Actually, it arrived on the local freight a few days after we moved in. The L. H. Manning Company furnished small four-lid stoves that could be rented for fifty cents a month. They were not very good stoves, and it was hard to control the heat, especially in the meager ovens. Our large kitchen range made things much easier for Mother—but not for Rey and me. The job of keeping it supplied with fuel fell to us.

House, lights, and fuel for foremen and track laborers were furnished by the railroad. Housing was primitive. Kerosene lamps and lanterns were the only source of light. Fuel consisted of old railroad ties and coal, and the railroad was stingy with the coal. After all, the railroad had to buy it and ship it and made no profit from it. The foreman always took half of all the coal delivered. The rest was dumped into a bin to be shared by our family and the families of the three or four other track laborers on the section gang. Old railroad ties, on the other hand, were plentiful, and all they required was muscle to cut them into stove-size chunks. The railroad furnished the tools for this: single-bit axes and two-man crosscut saws.

Keeping that old kitchen range supplied with wood seemed like a major chore. Mother's cry of "Boys, the wood box is empty!" was something we came to hear in our sleep.

When we complained about the never-ending chore, Mother merely said, "If you would fill the wood box completely early in the morning, you wouldn't have to do it again until supper time."

We tried, but what looked like a nearly full box to us looked like a nearly empty box to Mother. Actually, it wasn't too bad. Since we were aged only eight and seven that first winter (Rey's birthday came in December), Dad did all the wood cutting. All we had to do was haul it in and throw it into that wood box that we never seemed able to fill up.

There were a couple of other things that took getting used to. The first night in our new home, we children went to sleep on the floor in the west room. Suddenly we were awakened by the most frightful noise, and through the window above us we could see reflections of the very fires of hell. We rushed to the window to see what terrible thing had invaded our peace. What we saw were two engines chugging away at the head of a heavily loaded freight train. The long train passed slowly, and just behind the caboose came three more engines, helping to push the train uphill.

Fruit trains eastbound from California consisting of one hundred or more cars could be pulled by a single road engine on the flat Nevada desert.[1] But to climb the nine-mile hill from Wells to Moor took five engines. They were still on the grade when they passed our house and were still pushing with every ounce of power they had. The helper engines were uncoupled at Moor, turned around on the wye,[2] and returned all coupled together to Wells to wait for the next heavy freight. It took a night or two to get used to them; then we never heard them again in our sleep.

The other feature of our home to which we had to adjust was that outdoor privy. Even in warm weather, a privy is not the most pleasant place to go. But we had arrived at Moor in November. Dad had used an outdoor privy when he was a boy growing up in Mexico, and Mother was not unfamiliar with the detached outhouses used in many places in Denmark, even in the cities. The difference was that the weather in both Mexico and Denmark was milder, and the outhouses—at least the ones in Denmark—were much better built.

All the railroad privies leaked air. They were lightly built structures with all manner of cracks and crevices that let in the cold, and nighttime temperatures around zero degrees Fahrenheit were not unusual. The first thing you noticed when the wind blew (and at Moor the wind blew all the time) was that no matter the wind direction outside, inside the privy it was always blowing straight up. The only way to shut off that blast of cold air was to sit on it. What did we do when we had to answer the call of nature in the middle of the night with the temperature at zero or below and with wind and drifting snow? Every house in Moor had an article of furniture that in other parts of the country was fast disappearing from the American scene: the chamber pot under the bed.

Now there were several problems connected with using a chamber pot. For one thing, it had to be emptied by someone each morning. And when it got full, there always seemed to be someone who had to see if it wouldn't hold just a little more. A third problem was that it was always someone else's chore to carry it out and empty it, never the one who had overfilled it. And there was yet another problem that seemed to aggravate Mother more than any of the others: there was always someone whose aim wasn't too good.

Nevertheless, the chamber pot with all its problems was far better than going out to the privy in the middle of a winter night. Needless to say, etiquette demanded that if you had to make any more than a liquid deposit, you went out to the privy anyway, unless you were so sick you couldn't get out of bed by yourself. In our house, that battered old chamber pot inevitably was the subject of a number of animated discussions.

The first Monday after we moved to Moor, Rey, Grant, and I were introduced to another early American tradition that was steadily disappearing: the one-room school.

3

One-Room School

The Holborn school at Moor convened that first Monday we were in Moor, at nine in the morning upstairs in the Higley home. As the section foreman, Jess Higley had a large house with a spacious upstairs large enough to be used as a schoolroom. Although much larger than our tie house, the foreman's house was still primitive, having no running water or indoor plumbing. The name of the school, Holborn, had been chosen by the Higley children themselves at the beginning of the school year; they named the school in honor of a station on the railroad just seven miles east of Moor, where their maternal grandparents lived.

The school comprised a teacher and seven students. The teacher, Miss Herma Robison, was a pretty young woman from Metropolis, Nevada. This was her first teaching assignment. She was a likeable, outgoing girl who participated wholeheartedly in whatever activities were available in Moor and the surrounding countryside. I have an old snapshot of her dressed as a man, wearing bib overalls, a peaked wool cap, and a painted mustache. She is pretending to have a fistfight with Dad.

The students were the Higley children—Odell, Phyllis, Blain, and Doris—and the Call children—Rey, Grant, and I. Odell, at twelve, was the oldest; he was in seventh grade. Phyllis, ten, was in fifth grade, and Blain, nine, was in fourth grade. I was in third grade, Rey was in second grade, and Doris and Grant were in first grade. Although Grant and Doris were only five, Miss Robison wanted them in school to round out the student body.

The Daltons were the only other family with a school-age child, but Mrs. Dalton insisted that Moor's one-room school wasn't good enough for her daughter Doris, so she spent the school year in Ogden. We saw Doris Dalton, who was my age, only during the Christmas and summer vacations.[1] The railroad had promised to furnish an old passenger coach for use as a schoolroom, but it was slow in coming. When it finally arrived in late winter or early spring, it was spotted on a shoofly the section gang had built off a side track located east of all the houses in Moor.[2] We walked along the track to go to school. No one seemed to think this arrangement was particularly dangerous. After all, we lived around tracks and trains, didn't we?

The coach was very old, dating from the 1800s, and had a potbellied stove in each end. All of the passenger seats had been removed to make room for the desks. Odell was the janitor and maintained fires in the stoves during cold weather.

My education had begun at age six when I attended first grade at the Pingree School in Ogden. I was both beneficiary and victim of a series of experiments then being conducted in the city school system.

The Pingree School that year was experimenting with a new teaching system. The idea was to spend the entire school year concentrating on reading and learning to print letters and words. Arithmetic was to be taught beginning in the second year. In the first grade at the Pingree School, there was no such thing as an alphabet. Reading was taught using phonics. I remember meeting a girl of my own age who went to a different school. She asked me if knew my A-B-C's. I didn't know what she was talking about. When I was in the second grade I still didn't know the alphabet nor the names of the letters, yet my favorite book was an old *McGuffey's Fifth Reader,* which I read with ease.

About halfway through that first term, Dad bought a new house in a new residential section up on the East Bench, and I transferred to the Quincy school, which was not following the same system being used at Pingree. I didn't like the new neighborhood or the new school. Instead of going to school, I spent most days playing hooky. Of course, I was caught at it and brought back to school several times. Absence from school didn't seem to hurt my ability to read, but I learned nothing about arithmetic.

When I was ready to start the second grade, a new school on Polk Avenue opened its doors, and since we were in that district Rey, who was starting first grade, and I went to the Polk school. At the Polk school, they were experimenting with the platoon system. The teachers were specialized and stayed in their own rooms, while the students marched in formation from one classroom to another. In an entire school year, I didn't get to know any of the students or any of the teachers, and I did poorly in most subjects.

I still loved to read, but I hated arithmetic. I hadn't learned any of the simple addition or subtraction facts, and an assignment that most of my classmates could finish in a few minutes would take me what seemed like several boring hours—that is, if I could stand to spend that much time on it.

Usually I didn't bother. It was much easier just to write down any number that popped into my head, turn in the paper, and forget it. Surprisingly enough, some of the answers I had just guessed at turned out to be right—not many, but some. I don't recall a teacher ever asking how I had arrived at so many ridiculous answers—probably too busy to give it a thought.

I was starting an unproductive year in yet another school when we moved to Moor. I had done poorly in the large, impersonal city schools. But I thrived in the one- and two-room schools of Nevada.

Shortly after we arrived at Moor, Dad promised me five dollars if I would complete the third and fourth grades in one year and get promoted to the fifth grade. Herma Robison cooperated by giving me a number of assignments and classes in the fourth grade along with Blain. Arithmetic was a problem for me, but Miss Robison took considerable pains to drill me in the basic facts that every child was expected to learn. She appointed Phyllis as drill instructor, and Phyllis took her job very seriously. I hated the whole business, but I did try. I finally got to the point that I could give the answer to, say, seventeen-minus-nine or eight-times-seven with only a second or two's thought.

It was while we were in the passenger coach that Blain showed me how to cheat at spelling. "Look," he said, "all you have to do is write down the words on your desk, and then when the teacher gives us the words, just copy them."

Why I took his suggestion, I don't know. I didn't need to cheat. I already knew how to spell all the words. Naturally Miss Robison caught on—she was no dummy. She never said a word about it to either of us, but when we got our papers back with all our correctly spelled words, they were marked with a zero.

At the end of the school year, Blain and I were promoted to the fifth grade. I got my five dollars and managed to spend it over the course of the summer. I don't remember exactly how I did that, since there were no stores at Moor. Perhaps I ordered something from the Montgomery Ward catalog or spent it during some of my infrequent trips to Wells. Anyway, it was all gone by the end of summer.

Every student in the school except Doris and Grant got a report card showing that they had been promoted. Doris and Grant got nothing at all, not even a word of explanation. This disturbed Grant. In later years, he argued that he had worked hard and should have gotten something in return, so he made up his mind that school just wasn't worth the effort. For years afterward he had no use for school.

Did Herma Robison, out of misplaced sympathy, fudge just a little in promoting me to the fifth grade? I have often wondered, since I don't think I was doing fourth grade work in math. In any case, she didn't have to put up with me in the fifth grade—she didn't return to the Holborn school for the 1929–30 term.

4

Cabin Fever

It was the wind that bothered Mother the most that first winter. It blew constantly from the west and piled up the snow in huge drifts. The wind blew the snow over the edge of the cut where the little depot was located and piled up a drift that threatened to bury it.

At Anthony, a way station a mile east of the depot, where the double track ended, there was a set of electric switches that were operated from the depot at Moor. Power for the switches was supplied by "wet" batteries, called Edison cells, which were regenerated chemically by Ira Wines, the signal maintainer. Sweeping snow out of those switches was a constant chore for the section crew. To keep snow from filling the cuts and stopping all traffic, the railroad had built snow fences along the tops of the cuts. This kept down the heavy drifting and kept the cuts open, but it took only a little snow to foul the electric switches. There was lots of night work that winter, lots of overtime. As the winter wore on, people cooped up in small houses began to get cabin fever.

Cabin fever was a common complaint among people living in remote locations during the winter in the late nineteenth and early twentieth centuries, and Moor certainly qualified as a remote location.[1] Of course, it was possible to get away for a time. The trains ran, but a train trip involved at least an overnight stay somewhere. If a family had a car they could drive to Wells if the road, U.S. 40, happened to be open. (It frequently wasn't, due to drifting snow.) Things to do in Wells consisted of (a) walking up and down the single main street, (b) shopping at Quilici & Sons or one of the other meager stores, (c) going to the picture show if the theater happened to be open, and (d) going to church. For adults there were two other diversions: having a drink or gambling in one of the illegal saloons.

The Wells branch of the Church of Jesus Christ of Latter-Day Saints met in an ugly gray building that had once been a dance hall, situated on Main Street just a few doors west of the bank. We attended infrequently since we didn't have a car and went only when the Higleys invited us to go with them. They always invited us to go when they went, but they seldom went since Jess usually wasn't inclined, and when he was inclined he usually patronized the saloons while his family and the rest of us went to church.

Being cooped up inside for days and nights on end was beginning to get very boring, yet every time we stepped outside the door it was into a fresh snowdrift. About the middle of February we were all sick of it.

On Washington's Birthday, the weather at last turned mild and the wind quit. Since it was neither a workday nor a school day, Dad and Miss Robison proposed to hike to Wells to get the mail. They were fairly sure that they could get the postmaster to open the post office for them. Mr. Wines usually went to Wells on his motorcar and brought the mail up several times a week, but on this day he had gone to Ogden.

Was Dad afflicted with cabin fever, even though he spent his working days—and some nights—out in the cold and that almost-never-ending wind? He probably was, and with good reason. The little two-room tie house had, for us, shrunk to a single room. Uncle Glenn, one of Dad's younger brothers, had just gotten married and had come to Moor to work on the railroad. All of the houses assigned to the section crew were full, so we had to share our house with him and his bride, Aunt Elsie. There were eight of us living in that one room in the middle of the winter. I can well imagine that Dad wasn't looking forward to spending the holiday cooped up with six active, noisy children.

Dad and Miss Robison planned to leave early in the morning, walking along the track, and return by evening—an eighteen-mile round trip. When we heard about it, Rey, Blain, and I wanted to go, but Dad shook his head. "It's too far for you to walk, and I doubt that Miss Robison and I could carry you when you got tired."

After a brief huddle, we came up with another idea. "Well, then, can we hike to Holborn and visit Blain's grandpa and grandma? It's only seven miles, and we can stay all night and come back tomorrow. It's Saturday and no school." A conference took place between the two sets of parents, followed by a call on the company telephone to Holborn. It was decided that the three of us could go, but only if we agreed to stay off the tracks. We were to take the road that ran most of the way on the old abandoned Central Pacific Railroad grade.[2] So we promised to stay off the tracks. But before we could get started, there was a complication. Phyllis, Blain's older sister, announced that she was coming along.

At 6,200 feet above sea level, Moor is in the high desert. It sits at the top of a pass a mile and a half to two miles wide (today it is just off I-80, at Exit 360) covered with piñon, juniper, and sage. The double-track railroad winds its way up from Wells, nine miles to the west and a thousand feet lower, to Anthony, from which single track runs east to Holborn, Pequop, and beyond. Except for isolated ranches and the towns of Montello, Oasis, and Wendover, the entire area between Wells and the Utah line is an empty wilderness. Most of the little way stations scattered along the track at seven- to nine-mile intervals were once inhabited by railroad people and their families. Today, the people are gone, and the wilderness is absolute.

We all started out in the morning. Dad and Miss Robison went west, and we went east. It was a cloudy, mild day, and we made good time for the first half mile, until we got to the first of the old CPRR cuts. It was full of snow. We had to wade in deep snow or go around it by climbing the side of the cut. The next cut was also full of snow. At the third cut, Phyllis announced that she was going to hike the rest of the way on the tracks since they were free of snow. "You can all come with me. It's a lot easier than on this old road."

"We're supposed to stay on the road," Rey (who was generally the rebellious member of the family) righteously reminded us.

We all knew that walking on the ties along a single-track main line is dangerous. On a double track, we always walked facing traffic. On a single track, however, with trains rolling in both directions, it can be very unpleasant to learn how quietly a train can sneak up behind you. If the wind is blowing in the wrong direction you might not even hear the whistle the engineer is frantically blowing for you to get off the track. For a person walking the ties, the block signals indicating approaching trains were not much help, since they were too far apart to do a walker much good.[3]

"Wendell, why don't you come with me, and we'll race to see which way is the fastest?"

When I hesitated, she shrugged and walked off toward the forbidden tracks. I reluctantly followed, knowing that I was already in trouble with Dad, who took a dim view of any sort of disobedience. After a moment, Rey and Blain continued along the old roadbed.

The hike along the tracks took Phyllis and me most of the day. She was in no hurry, and we had to stop and rest a lot. I don't remember any trains. There must have been trains going in both directions, but since we didn't have any narrow escapes, I just don't remember them. After all, avoiding trains was something we did almost daily, pretty much without thinking about it. Usually they were easy to see and avoid. The smoke from the engine would show up over a hill or around a curve, and on a still day it was possible to hear the rails singing ahead of an approaching train.

Finally, as the short winter day came to a close, we arrived at the pump station located a mile west of Holborn. The railroad had installed a water tank for watering engines, which drew water from a nearby spring. There was a gas engine-driven pump, and an old man with a bad foot whose job it was to operate the pump and keep the tank full.

"I've walked as far as I'm going to!" Phyllis declared. "Let's get the old man to give us a ride the rest of the way on his speeder."

"It's only a mile," I replied. "We can make it."

"I'm tired, my feet hurt, and besides, I'm cold."

She marched up to the old man's door and knocked. "Hello, Phyllis," he said when he opened the door. "Haven't seen you around here for some time! Just what are you up to?"

Suddenly, she looked terribly tired, forlorn, and just about ready to cry. "We're trying to get to my grandma's house. We've come a long way. We're awfully tired, and it's getting dark. Please, could you take us the rest of the way on the speeder?"

The old man looked at her. She managed to look a little worse. He shook his head, put on his coat and cap, and wrestled the speeder onto the track. The speeder was a three-wheeled vehicle, correctly called a velocipede, intended to carry one person.[4] It was operated by pumping a large lever forward and back. The operator's feet were braced on the lower end of the lever, below the fulcrum, so that the feet pressed forward as the lever was pulled back.

Finally, after dark, Phyllis and I arrived at Holborn, ignominiously perched on the back of the speeder pumped by that crippled old man. Rey and Blain had been there for hours. They had run the last mile or so through shallow drifts just to make sure that they got there first. The grandparents had been in touch with the parents, and all of them were beginning to worry. After all, it was totally empty country with no shelter at all, and we had been hiking on the forbidden main line. They were about to put a motorcar on the track and start looking for us when we showed up. Dad and Miss Robison, in the meantime, had caught a ride back from Wells with a friendly engineer on a helper.[5]

The next day, Jess Higley and his section crew rode the motorcar over to Holborn and gave us a ride home.[6] Such things were strictly against company rules, and we were cautioned to say nothing about it. Later that day, my dreaded interview with Dad took place.

"I'm sorry I walked on the tracks," I told him.

"I've talked to Rey, and he told me what happened," he said. "Sometimes a man has to decide between two choices, neither of them very good. I think you made the better one. It would never do to let Phyllis go by herself. I do feel bad about that poor old man having to give two perfectly healthy kids a ride on his speeder, though. He's so weak and crippled up, he can scarcely get that thing on and off the track. Aren't you just a little ashamed about that?" I admitted I was. "Well," Dad admitted, "there probably wasn't a whole lot you could have done about that either."

And that was the end of it. It was also the end of our bout with cabin fever.

During the trip from the pump station to Holborn with Phyllis and me on the speeder, the old man had tried to make a joke about the fast, westbound daily mail train. "That Number 9 is a good train," he chuckled. "If it hits anybody, it never hurts them—it just kills them all!"

A year or two later, when the old man was a bit slow in getting his speeder off the track, he was hit by a fast train and killed. I never learned what train it was. It may even have been that "good train," Number 9.

The water tank and pump house are gone now. The buildings at Holborn are gone, although the sign is still there. The last time I was there looking around, I couldn't even find the spring.[7]

5

Grant's Mountain

The first week in May 1929, school let out for the summer. The small schools in Nevada operated for only eight months rather than nine, as in the larger schools. Not that we minded in the least—we were free for four glorious months!

One bright, cloudless day in May, we decided to climb Grant's Mountain to see what was on the other side. Grant's Mountain lies parallel to the track about a mile or a mile and a half to the north of Moor; it is the first, or southernmost, of the Windemere Hills. Grant's Mountain is not its official name. As far as I have been able to determine, it has no name. In our family there are two stories telling how the ridge got its name, each with its advocates who insist that their version is the right one.

The story Mother used to tell goes like this: Grant, who was six at the time, was making a big fuss one day because one of the other children had gotten some little trinket and Grant thought he was being left out.

"Nobody ever gives me anything," he sobbed, with the tears running down his face. "I just never get anything!"

Dad took it just about as long as he could. Finally he said, "Grant, come on outside."

Outside, Dad pointed to the prominent hill: "See that mountain over there? Well, you may have it. Now I don't ever want to hear anymore about no one giving you anything. You now own the mountain!"

Rey, however, insists that the following version is the correct one, as he maintains he was there when it happened: Dad came home from work one day in a jocular mood (that was not unusual; he was nearly always pleasant when he got home) and said to Mother, "See that mountain over there? How would you like to have it for your very own?"

"My goodness!" Mother exclaimed. "I don't have any use for a mountain! What in the world would I do with a mountain?"

"I want it!" Grant, who was standing nearby, piped up quickly before anyone else could get in a claim. "I'll take it! Please, can I have it?" So Dad gave it to him. It has been Grant's Mountain ever since.

We started out for Grant's Mountain, Rey, Grant, Dale, and I. Our little sister Adona, who had just turned three, thought she was big enough to go, so, with Mother's permission, we took her along. We hadn't been gone long—perhaps two hours—when Mother began to worry about Adona. She began to regret letting us take her, and she became so agitated that she went out to look for us.

In the meantime, we had climbed the face of the mountain, gotten to the top, played in some snowdrifts still left over from winter on the north slope, walked west along the ridge, and dropped over onto the north side among some big old piñon trees. By then we were tired and didn't feel like climbing back up to the top of the mountain, so we decided to walk around the west end, since it looked like it was so close. By then, Adona was so tired she could scarcely move, so I carried her on my back.

It took longer to get home going around the mountain than we thought it would; we arrived home tired, hungry, and thirsty in the middle of the afternoon. I had carried Adona nearly every step of the way home. When we got home, Mother was gone. We didn't know where she was, but we started to rustle up what food we could find. We built up the fire and fried some eggs, which we ate with bread and milk. I was so tired by then that I just lay down on a convenient bed and went to sleep.

When Mother finally came home, frustrated and exhausted from her fruitless search, she found her three-year-old daughter standing on a chair in front of the stove, frying herself an egg. I was fast asleep, and apparently no one else would do it for her.

* * *

It was a splendid summer. We hiked over the Wood Hills to the south, climbed to the top of 7,000-foot Over Peak and looked east across Independence Valley to the Pequop Mountains. We had never heard the name Independence Valley. Odell named it "Sagebrush Flat." I still think his was the better name. We built a hut out of railroad ties in a little swale Odell named Eagle Hollow. We made rubber guns and cut up old inner tubes for ammunition.

We made root beer, and then had to wait four interminable days for the fizz to develop. We put the bottle caps on the rail for the trains to flatten out, so we could use them as play money. This practice came to a sudden halt when the reflection of one of the caps caught an engineer in the eye and nearly gave him heart failure. Dad said the reflection from the sun made the bottle cap look as big as a house.

We found torpedoes and fastened them to telegraph poles and threw rocks at them until they exploded.[1] Dad frequently cautioned us to be careful with them. He told us about the time he had been standing with a group of men around a torpedo that was lying on a tie. One of the men reached across the rail and hit the torpedo with a heavy steel bar used for aligning track. Everyone standing in the circle was hit by flying rocks, even though the torpedo had been on the tie, not on the ballast between the ties. Years later, after we had left Moor, we heard that Doris Dalton had placed a torpedo on a rail and hit it with a hammer. Particles of powder and torpedo casing sprayed into her face, marking her for life.

As the Fourth of July approached, we planned to have a spectacular fire to celebrate. We spent days walking up and down the track looking for fusees that had not burned completely. By the time the Fourth arrived, we had nearly a hundred partially burned fusees.[2] When it got dark on the night of the Fourth, we built a small fire of wood and then piled on our fusees. The result was magnificent. The red glare from those burning fusees could be seen for miles—and that was our undoing. Both Dad and Jess Higley came running.

"You've built your fire much too close to the tracks," Dad said. "It'll scare those poor engineers to death. Some of those old men have weak hearts!" Higley directed us to put the fire out. Now a fusee fire, as we then found, is hard to put out. We managed it finally, by burying our fire under about two feet of dirt. By then, nearly all the fusees were exhausted anyway.

It was during the summer that Dad took his examination and qualified as a foreman, and right away he began serving at various sections as a relief foreman. While he worked as a relief foreman he received foreman's pay. The rest of the time he earned pay as a track laborer at about thirty cents an hour. His assignments were usually for a week or two, occasionally as long as a month. As the railroad did not provide paid vacations, a day off meant loss of a day's pay. When a foreman had to take time off, it was usually for as short a time as he could manage.

Dad kept a large steamer trunk loaded with his "baching outfit," ready to go at a moment's notice. His personal equipment included a brand-new, sixty-five-dollar, twenty-one-jewel, lever-set Hamilton watch, which the railroad required him to provide for himself. It was a beautiful timepiece with a platinum case. I'm not sure if the railroad required the platinum case, but the size of the watch, the number of jeweled bearings, and the lever-set arrangement were definitely required.[3]

Overwhelmed by Dad's new status, I once bragged to Blain Higley, "My Dad has to be the best foreman on the railroad because he can talk Spanish to the men." It just had to be true, I thought, since most of the section hands in those days were Hispanic, and most of them spoke little or no English.[4]

"Don't you believe it," Blain retorted. "My dad don't talk Spanish, but he can swear at them and make them hurry!"

Occasionally, if the relief period was a short one, Dad would take Rey or me with him. I recall once spending a few days with him when he was relief foreman at Tulasco, just west of Wells. Why he was there, I never found out. Tulasco was a section on the Western Pacific, not the SP.

Some small events will stick in a person's memory down through the years and remain vivid far beyond any significance they might have had at the time. I remember one day that summer when two lady schoolteachers from the East stopped to get a little water for their car, which was overheating. The nearby transcontinental highway, U.S. 40 (now I-80), was nothing more than a graded gravel road, and there was very little traffic. It was a big event when any of the infrequent cars stopped. The teachers got out to let their engine cool down and stretch a bit. Looking to the West, they saw the tops of the Ruby Mountains behind Wells. Although it was July, the 11,000-foot peaks shone white and bright in the sun.

One of the ladies stared at the mountains for a moment and then turned and said, "Is that snow on top of those mountains or is it beach sand?"

Every three months the supply train would come out from Ogden to leave supplies required by the railroad crews and pick up scrap. We liked the supply train because of the magnet. Usually the train came during the day when we were in school, but in the summer we were on hand to watch. The magnet fascinated us. One car of the train held a gasoline engine-driven crane with a big, round electromagnet on the end of the cable instead of a hook or bucket.

We would watch as the magnet picked up huge piles of old spikes, tie plates, angle bars, brake shoes, and anything else that a tidy section crew had picked up along the right-of-way and brought back to the scrap heap near the toolhouse. Hanging from each load of scrap was usually a long string of spikes held in place by the magnetic force. The crane would swing over a gondola car, or "gon," positioned just ahead of or behind the crane car, and then the magnet would drop the load to land in the bottom of the gon with a satisfying crash.

When the small scrap had all been cleaned up, the magnet began picking up scrap rails. The rails had been measured and marked by the section crew, and positioned so that the centers of the rails were aligned. The magnet could pick up two full-length rails at a time—a load of more than three tons. The rails were dropped with a crash into a gon at the opposite end of the crane car, but the rails were not dropped as far as the small scrap was.

The apparent boss of the supply train was not the conductor but the roadmaster, Mr. C. C. Clark. We watched Mr. Clark only from a distance. Jess Higley was always a bit nervous in the presence of the roadmaster, who was his immediate boss; he was nervous even talking about him when the roadmaster wasn't there. Inevitably we children sensed this nervousness, and we always kept far away from the roadmaster so we wouldn't be noticed.

He was a short, bandy-legged man with a big belly who always wore a black suit and a white shirt. No matter how hot the weather, we never saw him with his suit jacket off, and in the summer heat he would pace restlessly about, smoking the stub of a cigar. We were sure he was some sort of an ogre hired by the railroad to frighten section crews and their children.

Of less interest, but still important, was the weekly local freight. Except for fresh milk, which arrived on one of the daily passenger trains, all groceries and other necessities came on the local. The local also delivered water for the two cisterns. One of the cisterns was located east of the depot, for use by the station agent, second and third trick operators, and signal maintainer; the second one was located in front of Higley's house. Although there was a small spring located about two miles up in the Wood Hills, the railroad didn't take advantage of it. Water was shipped in a tank car and dumped into the two cisterns. The cisterns were equipped with hand pumps, and all we had to do to get water was to work the pump handle up and down.

Much too soon, summer came to an end. In September, the day after Labor Day, another school year got under way.

6

Parmel

Herma Robison didn't come back for the next school year. We had a new teacher, Parmel Higley, a sister-in-law of Jess's. It didn't take me long to discover that I didn't like her. The first day of school she put both Blain and me back into the fourth grade. In time she managed to get herself disliked by every student in the school, including her own nieces and nephews. Parmel was not a great teacher. She was meticulous, for instance, in giving assignments, but seldom praised anyone for good work. Mostly, she found fault with us.

At the beginning of the school year in September 1929, the railroad had still not delivered the promised coach, so we started school in a one-room shack normally used to house section hands. It was located just a few yards west of our tie house.

I recall a day in early September, in school in the little house. We were having our weekly class in art. Even though the door was open in an effort to augment the light coming in through the two tiny windows, the room was gloomy. The contrast with the light from the bright afternoon sun reflecting from the gray-yellow dirt outside the door made the inside of the makeshift schoolhouse seem even darker. I was painting with watercolors, and I was having fun. Parmel stood at my shoulder for a moment, and then asked, "What color are you using to paint that grass?"

"Green," I said. "The grass is green."

"You're using black," she admonished. "You're painting that grass black!"

Well, I knew it was green. True, the light in that little room wasn't very good, but I had dipped my brush in green paint, and it had to be green! So I retorted, "Your eyes must not be very good, then." Without any warning, her hard palm exploded on the side of my face, and for a few seconds the room went black, except for a lot of little lights. Adults, especially teachers, didn't take much from children in those days.

When my tears had dried, I could see that in fact there was a lot of black drying in my green grass, and as it dried it seemed to get even blacker. At that point I decided that I couldn't paint. For the next several years I refused to try anything more artistic than pencil sketches. That slap in the face had been a powerful persuader.

My brother Grant started school repeating the first grade. Although he was now six and of school age, he was no longer interested in school. School was a place where you worked your heart out for nothing, so why work at all? Parmel dismissed him as a slow learner and paid little attention to him. For the next several years he did poorly. Teachers thought he wasn't very bright, and he didn't care. All that changed, however, when he entered the seventh grade. Years later, he told me that his teacher, Miss McQuiston, put her arm around him, hugged him, and told him that she was sure he could do better. So he did better—much better. He went from the bottom of his class to the top in less than two months.

The railroad delivered the coach to Moor a few weeks after school started and spotted it at the end of the wye. To get to school, we had to cross the tracks and walk about a half mile through the piñon, juniper, and sagebrush. Very soon we had cut an easy-to-follow trail, the beginning of which led through a part of the yard favored by Mrs. Higley's chickens. And that became a problem for Rey.

Higley's rooster didn't like Rey. The chickens were not confined in a run or coop but roamed about the yard. Every time Rey started on his way to school, there was that rooster, head down and wings outspread, daring him to take one more step. If it wasn't standing there blocking the trail, it would spy him from clear across the yard and run at him squawking. Rey was too terrified to cross Higley's yard by himself, so he would get Dale to go with him and chase the rooster away. Dale was only five and didn't go to school, but he wasn't afraid of the rooster.

Finally Dad decided that the foolishness had gone on long enough. "It's absolutely ridiculous," he said, "for a sixty-pound boy to be bullied by a six-pound chicken!"

He gave Rey a stick and told him to use it on the rooster. Yet even with the stick in his hand, Rey was afraid to tackle the bird. So Dad got another stick and told Rey, "You start whacking the rooster, and I'll start whacking you!"

Rey had no choice, because Dad started right in. What followed next was something to see. Here came the rooster, dodging this way and that, wings outspread and squawking in terror . . . and here came Rey swinging his stick at the rooster and yelling in pain . . . and here came Dad, swinging his stick at Rey and muttering under his breath. It was just too much for that rooster. It ran under Higley's garage and stayed there for the rest of the day. From then on, whenever Rey showed up in the yard, the rooster found some urgent business under the garage or on the other side of Higley's house.

Parmel did introduce one daily event that I enjoyed. Every day after lunch she would read to us for fifteen minutes. She read stories of humor, adventure, and mystery. Among them were Mark Twain's *The Adventures of Tom Sawyer,* Eleanor Porter's *Pollyanna,* and Frances Hodgson Burnett's *The Secret Garden.* Those first fifteen minutes right after lunch were the bright spot of the whole school day. They must have been the only bright spot, since I don't remember anything else that took place during that term.

Snow began falling in November, and the ever-blowing wind soon piled it up against the snow fences. The drift between our tie house and the woodpile and the outhouse began to grow. A trip to the outhouse or the woodpile often started with a bit of shovel work. Why didn't we save some of that work by piling the wood against the side of the house? I don't know, but apparently nobody along the railroad ever did that. It may have been forbidden by the railroad as a possible fire hazard.

It seems in retrospect that we may have lived during those winters with almost constant fire hazards. In order to keep warm, it was often necessary to build up a fire in the heating stove to the point that the stove glowed red, and the stovepipe along with it. We did eliminate one hazard, however, during that winter.

Early one morning—perhaps four or five hours after midnight—we awoke to a heavy pounding on the door. When Dad opened the door, there stood President Edward White of the Wells branch of the Church of Jesus Christ of Latter-Day Saints.

"Thank God, you're all right!" he said shakily, smiling in relief as he came in.

"Of course we are," Dad responded, offering him one of our few chairs. "What seems to be the problem?"

"I had the most horrible dream! It was so vivid, I woke up in a panic. I dreamed that one of your children was starting a fire in a stove, using kerosene to get it going, when it exploded, and your house burned with all of you inside! I drove up here thinking that all I would see would be a pile of ashes. I'm so glad you're OK!"

"Well," Dad said, "we all seem to be healthy. Thank you so much for your concern. And if it will relieve your mind, I promise you that—although we have used kerosene to start fires in the past—we will never do it again. Won't you stay for breakfast?"

It was true. One of the problems with starting a fire was chopping the kindling fine enough to burn readily. We had gotten a little lazy, and it was much more convenient just to throw a few sticks of wood onto the grate, with or without paper under them, soak them with kerosene, and light a match. There was always plenty of kerosene; the railroad furnished it for free to use in our lamps. In a cold stove, that practice usually was safe enough, but if there were a few hot coals in the grate, they could vaporize some of the kerosene to create a mixture as explosive as gasoline.

Dad told us that President White's dream was a warning from the Lord, and that one warning was all we needed. No more kerosene for starting fires! I have since wondered, if it was a warning from the Lord as Dad insisted it was, why didn't the Lord just tell him directly instead of President White? It has occurred to me that it might not have had the same impact as pulling that poor man out of bed on a wintry night and sending him nine miles up the hill in the snow and cold.

School ended for the year at the end of the first week of May 1930, and a few weeks later the Call family moved from Moor. Jess Higley remained foreman at Moor until he retired from the railroad. However, after U.S. 40 was paved and improved, he moved to Wells, and thereafter drove up to Moor to work.

* * *

Moor is empty now. The buildings and the wye are gone. The wide place in the cut where the little depot was located is empty. The little three-foot piñon tree that stood in front of the Higleys' house next to the tracks has grown so tall the linemen have had to cut off the top to keep it out of the telegraph wires. All that is left of our tie house is a trace of ashes and two concrete ramps where the doors used to be. Except for Odell, who lives in New York and Florida, and Joanne, who was born after we left Moor, the Higleys have all passed on.

Grant's Mountain is still there, of course, and Dad's numerous descendants always point it out when they drive past it on I-80.

"There's Grant's Mountain!" they shout. And then they repeat the stories of how it got its name.

Recently, on a sunny October day, I climbed the west shoulder of Grant's Mountain. Scattered among outcroppings of chalcedony and quartz were stands of small piñon and juniper. I was surprised to see that the Chinese woodcutting crews the railroad had employed during the late 1800s to provide fuel for the wood-burning engines had cut trees right to the top of the ridge, but hadn't touched the trees on the north slope. Some of those old stumps were nearly three feet in diameter. How tall would a piñon tree with a three-foot-thick trunk be? Some of the old trees on the north slope appeared to be more than twenty feet tall, but I didn't see any with a trunk the size of those the woodcutting crews had harvested.

From the top of the mountain I could see where the Higleys' house and our tie house used to stand and the site of the little house Parmel taught school in. I sat on a stump and watched a freight train of nearly a hundred cars as it labored up the grade from Wells. The diesel electric road engine was having no trouble pulling the train up the hill. It would have taken five heavy steam engines, two pulling and three pushing, to move that train when we lived there. That diesel was efficient and economical—but the excitement was gone.

7

Learning to Swim in the Desert

In June 1930, the Call family moved from Moor to Comus in Humboldt County in north-central Nevada. Although we would miss Grant's Mountain and the junipers and piñon pines that grew around Moor, Comus had something even more attractive—a river. Not just any river, but that infamous desert river, the Humboldt.

The Humboldt River—a raging torrent in the spring, a bare trickle in the summer—was called by western historian Dale Morgan the "most hated river in America."[1] But with its treacherous, ever-shifting bottom, crumbling banks, and changing channels, it held a hazardous attraction for us boys. Dad and Mother took pains to point out the dangers this notorious stream posed for children, but the river was close—just across the tracks—and we were drawn to it like flies to flypaper.

Comus doesn't exist anymore. The railroad has removed the buildings, torn up the side track, and taken down the sign. The site is about thirty-five miles west of Battle Mountain and a few miles east of Golconda. Situated at the northern tip of a spur of the Sonoma Range, it can be reached by a dirt road built on the original Central Pacific Railroad grade running east from Emigrant Canyon.

The only existing features to identify the site that can be seen from this road are the truss bridge on the north, or eastbound, Union Pacific track and an old round concrete telephone booth on the south, or westbound, Southern Pacific track. Dad was serving as relief foreman at Comus on the Southern Pacific, relieving a man who had gone to Italy for the summer.

The day we arrived, Dad called his four older boys together in the bare living room of the foreman's house. (The permanent foreman had removed all his furniture and personal effects, and the meager possessions we had brought with us from the tie house at Moor didn't begin to fill this bigger house.)

"Boys, I think it is time you learned to swim."

"Yay-y-y!"

"When do we start?"

"Today?"

"Right now?" Some of us were already heading for the door.

"Now just hold on a minute! Let me tell you what we are going to do! You are not going to run pell-mell down to the river. You will only get yourselves drowned. We must have a little order here!" Reluctantly, we went back to our places and waited for what was to come next.

"That river is very dangerous. In the afternoons when I get home from work, I will take you down to the river to swim. In the meantime, you must promise me that you will not go near the river until I decide you can swim safely."

With the Humboldt River practically in our front yard, the only way to keep from losing one or more children short of locking us all up in the house was for Dad to teach us to swim. Even that was not a perfect solution, since it was said that several good swimmers had lost their lives in the river's murky depths. However, swimming lessons combined with daily prayers for our safety was the best move our parents could make. So we gave our word that we would stay away from the river.

The river at this point zigzags between the two railroads. A bend in the river channel brought the river right up to the embankment on the north side of the SP tracks. Just across from the foreman's house, it turned north toward the Western Pacific (now the Union Pacific) track. From the house we could look north along the channel to the far bend where it turned west out of sight. The water in the near bend, just across the track from our house, was too shallow for swimming. Walking down the riverbed to the next bend, the one by the WP track, we found the water was deep enough.

So after work that summer, Dad would walk with us down the riverbed to the far bend and give us swimming lessons. We would spend all day waiting for him to come home so we could go swimming. It was a long, hot wait. Eventually, though, we would hear the motorcar coming along the track. It would stop in front of the toolhouse, and the men would pile off, manhandle it off the track, roll it into the toolhouse, and lock up. By then, we were more than ready to get in the water.

In June that year, the water in the river was still quite swift, but only ankle deep in the channel between the two bends in the river. There was still a fast-moving current in the bend where we were learning to swim. But we were safe. Dad was with us.

Now I had absolute faith in Dad's ability as a swimming instructor to watch over four active boys and keep us out of trouble. Once, before I could swim even a stroke, I was wading out in the channel with the water up to my neck. I lost my footing and the current started to sweep me away into a part of the river we knew was over our heads. I was floating face down in the water, but not horizontal; my feet were dragging lower down. I didn't panic. I knew that my head and the upper part of my back were above water, and I was certain that Dad would see me and come to my rescue.

After a few seconds floating like that, I began to need a breath of air, but Dad still hadn't come to me. A few more seconds, which seemed like minutes, and I was in distress. In desperation, I put my feet down—and touched bottom! I stood up and the water was only chest deep. That deep place we had been careful to avoid had disappeared. I looked over at Dad. All he did was grin. He had had confidence that I would work out my problem by myself. Once I had learned not to panic when my face went under water, it didn't take long to learn to swim.

The first thing Dad taught us to do was swim on our backs. Back swimming was easy. As long as we could stay on our backs and paddle a little, we could breathe and stay afloat indefinitely. However, before we were really good at it, we had a chance to demonstrate in front of strangers.

Shortly after we arrived at Comus, the foreman at Valmy, the next section to the east, told Dad that there was a hot spring north of Valmy that was large enough to bathe in. Since we didn't have a car, he offered to come get us the following Sunday and take us to the spring for a swim and a picnic. So the next Sunday, we went swimming in the Hot Pot.

The spring was on the side of a low hill a few feet above the alkali flat eight miles north of Valmy and a couple of miles northeast of the WP track. The pool was approximately round, perhaps twenty feet in diameter. One side was shallow with a gradually sloping bottom for a few feet out; then the bottom sloped abruptly down to a steep chimney. The water was very clear. From the bank where the slope was very steep, it seemed that we could see far down that chimney. Dad tried to dive down to see how deep the chimney ran, but he didn't get far. The water got too hot, he said.

The Valmy foreman had strung a rope across the spring to fence off the shallow end from the deep part to keep children and nonswimming adults from getting in over their heads. It seemed that of the half dozen adults in the party, Dad and Mother were the only ones who could swim. When asked if any of the children could swim, Dad had me go beyond the rope and show how I could swim on my back. I was able to swim alongside the rope for perhaps fifteen feet. Everyone applauded.

After the trip to the Hot Pot, we continued with our swimming lessons. However, Rey and I were dissatisfied. We weren't getting in enough swimming practice. It was our opinion that we ought to go swimming every day. Dad, on the other hand, thought that two or three sessions a week were about right. Rey and I couldn't stand to miss even one day down at the river, so we decided to do a little practicing on our own.

We found a place a bend or two to the west from where Dad took us. It was shielded by willows from the SP track. Although it was dangerous, we weren't complete fools. We carefully explored the river bottom with a long stick to make sure there weren't any deep holes before we started to practice our swimming. At least we practiced part of the time. Mostly we just played in the water. Still, we must have made considerable progress. One evening I overheard Dad mention to Mother, "I must be the best swimming instructor in the country. It is amazing how fast those boys are learning to swim, especially Wendell and Rey!"

One day as Rey and I were playing in our secret swimming hole, Rey stepped off into a hole we didn't know was there. Whether it was a hole newly created by the river, or a hole we had missed during our first exploration, I don't know. It wasn't really deep; the water came just to the top of his head as he stood on the bottom. He stood there with his hands waving in the air above the water. I stood on the edge of the hole and grabbed one of his hands. With the other hand he took hold of my wrist, and I began to pull him out.

The water at the edge of the hole was about chest deep on me. The bottom was sandy and a bit soft, and as I pulled, I could feel the edge of the hole start to break away under my feet. For a second or two I didn't know whether Rey was coming out or I was going in. Fortunately, before the whole edge of the hole gave way, he came out.

"Why didn't you just start swimming on your back?" I asked.

"I was scared and didn't think of it," he retorted.

Well, we were both scared. It scared us so badly that we didn't go back to our secret swimming place for nearly three days. Not long afterward, Dad found out what we had been doing. He came home one afternoon looking very solemn and greeted us with the words, "Well, what have you boys been doing that you shouldn't have?"

Rey and I looked at each other, and then, to Dad's great surprise, we confessed that we had been swimming without him. As it turned out, he had had something else entirely on his mind. I don't believe I ever found out what it was. I don't remember any punishment or any restrictions following our admission of disobedience. We learned to swim that summer, and we had no fear of the river. We did have a healthy amount of respect for it, however, and ever after we approached the Humboldt with caution.

From time to time in the years following, we would hear of accidents and people drowning in its unpredictable waters. One of the victims was a girl we knew who lived in Beowawe. Adele Bianca was a year or two older than I. She was an excellent swimmer, but she drowned in the Humboldt River at age seventeen.

Recently, on one cool morning in May, my brother Cyril and I visited the Hot Pot. So many years had gone by since we spent that Sunday afternoon there that I wasn't sure if it really existed or if I had dreamed it all. Cyril didn't remember anything about it as he was only two that first time. After a fair amount of wandering about over alkali flats and through stands of greasewood, we found the spring. It looked very much as I remembered it, except the water was turbid instead of clear, and there was a lot of trash scattered around the edge of the pool. A man who was swimming in the pool with his wife told us that he had cleaned up the site just a year before and had hauled away several pickup loads of trash. Of course, he had no way of removing the items that had been thrown into the deep chimney, the garbage that had turned the water from crystal clear to a murky brown.

"We come over here from Winnemucca as often as we can. But look at it now," he said, shaking his head. "The place is just as bad as it was before I cleaned it up."

We looked sadly at the array of old tires, broken glass, empty beer cans, discarded boxes, and other leavings. A pair of concrete piers that had once held a diving board stood forlornly on the bank overlooking the deep end of the pool. The Valmy Hot Pot, unique in its desert setting, off the beaten track and difficult to get to, had been exploited and abused. Some people obviously had cared about it, but just as obviously, others hadn't.

8

Shoshone

With the arrival of August, Dad and Mother were planning another move. The Comus section foreman was due home in a few weeks, and we would have to give him back his house.

"Why don't we just move into the house next door?" Rey asked. "It's empty, and it's big enough; then we could just stay here."

"It won't do," Dad replied. "There's no school here, and the state of Nevada will not set up a school for only three students."

Since school was furthest from our thoughts, my brothers and I left them to their problem and ran out to play. We were still enjoying the summer, spending most of the daylight hours down in the river. The stream in the channel had shrunk until it was a bare trickle zigzagging down a sandy course in the riverbed. Several times a day during our play in the fenced-off section yard, someone would suggest, "Let's go swimming!"

We would race to the front porch of the foreman's house, take off our clothes, and run across the tracks, slip down the riverbank, and run down the channel to the far bend, where there was still enough water to swim. We always swam naked, and since we were completely alone during the day, the front porch was the logical place to leave our clothing. On the rare occasions when anyone else was around, or if a train was coming, we would wait until they were gone before we headed for the river.

Dad warned us that there were rattlesnakes in the area, but we never ran across one. The only snake we saw was the dead rattler Dad brought home one day just to show us what they were like.

For the most part that summer we were completely happy. The long summer days seemed to go on forever. Oh, there were a few squabbles. Once Grant threw a glazed ceramic doorknob at Rey and hit him in the middle of the back. It broke the doorknob. I don't remember what Rey had done to Grant, but whatever it was, Grant obviously felt justified in throwing the doorknob.

That was also the summer we stopped talking Danish. From the time we were small, Mother had always spoken to us in Danish. She thought it would be good for her children to grow up knowing two languages, and at first it worked out very well. We played in English, but all the serious communication necessary to manage home and family was in Danish. To maintain his status as head of the household, Dad had to learn Danish to communicate with his children.

At Comus, we were almost completely isolated. The only other residents were single Mexican track laborers, who carried on their conversations in Spanish. So, as we children played together, if we didn't have an English word to get an idea across, we would substitute a Danish or a Spanish word. One day Mother overheard Dale and Grant in their play mixing English, Spanish, and Danish in the same sentence. Horrified, she called us all together.

"Beginning right now," she declared, "we will speak only English in this house. We will all speak English and speak it correctly. No more Danish and no more Spanish!"

It may have taken us a week or two to get used to the new rule, but we managed; the Danish language was gradually forgotten. But Spanish, because it was so prevalent, stayed with us.

As September approached, Dad began making calls to various sections to the east and west to find a place for us, one where we could go to school. He located a man who had not only an opening on his section, but also two daughters of school age and no school in which to enter them. These two, together with the three Call boys, would meet Nevada's minimum requirements to establish a school. So, by the end of August 1930, we had moved to Shoshone in northern Eureka County.

Shoshone doesn't exist anymore. The site is right at the Dunphy Interchange, Exit 254, off I-80. Dunphy itself, however, is located approximately two miles to the north and east, where the old highway, U.S. 40, crosses the Union Pacific track. When we moved there, U.S. 40 was a gravel road just outside the Southern Pacific fence. Charlie Helton was foreman of the Shoshone section. He had a fat wife, two daughters, and a collie dog.

On the first Tuesday of September, we enrolled in our second one-room school.

Dunphy school convened in a tiny one-room shack built to house track laborers without families. It had a bare wooden floor, a door, and two small windows. A potbellied SP company space heater stood in the center of the room. The light inside was bad enough to make reading difficult, so in warm weather the door was left open to let in more light. The teacher was Miss Dorothy McDonald, whose home was in Lovelock. At ten, I was in fifth grade, and the oldest student in school. Rey was in fourth grade, Lorraine Helton was in third grade, Grant was in second grade, and Marie Helton was in first.

Equipment for the school was meager. There weren't enough desks, books, maps, paper, pencils, blackboards, chalk, or anything else. Until that year, the school had been located on the Dunphy Ranch. William J. "Bill" Mahoney, who managed the ranch for the Dunphy estate and whose children had been attending the school there, had sent his wife and children to San Francisco, where the children enrolled in parochial school. The little schoolhouse on the ranch now stood empty.

Dad and Charlie Helton visited Bill Mahoney to try to get the school equipment moved from the ranch to Shoshone.

"Absolutely not!" Mahoney informed them. "I built the school, and everything in it belongs to me. You can bring the teacher and the kids over here to use the school if you want to."

Dad was outraged. "Do you mean to tell us that the teacher and five children will have to walk over here and then walk back every day all winter long?"

"I don't care how they get here," Mahoney said. "None of this equipment will leave the ranch."

After some more discussion, Bill Mahoney relented to the extent of allowing a few of the shabbiest desks to be moved to Shoshone, making sure that Dad and Charlie Helton understood that the items were all his and that they would have to be returned at the end of the school year.[1] The desks that finally came over from the ranch were too small for Rey and me, so Dad made us a desk. It was a double desk patterned after the two-student desks common in schools in the early nineteenth century.

Miss McDonald boarded with the Heltons. She was a pretty girl who was teaching for the first time. The thing I remember most about her was that she loved her students. She would often kiss each student as he or she left school for the day—that is, she kissed those of us who would allow it. I was the oldest in the school, and kissing the teacher didn't seem like the thing for a ten-year-old boy to do. I remember, though, that after some time had passed I offered to let her kiss me just once. She did, and it was kind of nice.

Although she didn't have enough experience to spot and correct the trouble my brother Grant was having, I believe she was a good teacher working under very difficult conditions. With only a small poorly heated and poorly lighted room to teach in, almost no teaching aids, and few textbooks and supplies, she did remarkably well. For instance, she introduced me to grammar and the English language, and I loved it.

Her technique was simple. She gave me a fifth-grade grammar workbook. All she said was, "You may work through this book as fast as you like, but don't turn to a new page until you have finished and corrected the one you have started."

I was fascinated. At the top of each page was a humorous cartoon. The parts of speech, sentence construction, and other elements of the language were carefully demonstrated. There was no such nonsense as diagramming sentences. Each part of speech was clearly explained, and there were enough reinforcing exercises that diagramming would have been superfluous and confusing. I learned more about the English language that year than at any time since.

In addition to teaching, Miss McDonald was also the school custodian, coming early each school day to sweep out and light a fire in the potbellied stove. During the day, she taught as many as six subjects to five children, each of whom was in a different grade. Her evenings were spent correcting the children's work and planning for the next school day. The lack of supplies—pencils and paper, for instance—was a continuing problem. I now suspect that she may have purchased (and paid for out of her own pocket) some of the things we used.

The state of Nevada required music to be included in the curriculum. With severely limited facilities, most teachers conducted singing sessions. But Miss McDonald had her own ideas of what was appropriate. She had a small portable phonograph, and she had brought with her a number of popular records of the day. Some of these were single-sided records distributed in drugstores under the title "Hit of the Week." I recall part of one we used to sing; it went something like this:

This little pig went to market to buy himself some stock.
This little pig went home again with his system full of shock.
I don't understand their language, don't know what it's all about,
For the Bull buys up and the Bear sells down,
And the Broker sells you out!
CHORUS
And here is the song they sing the whole day long:
"Oh, the market's not so good today; your stock looks kind of sick.
In fact it all drops down a point each time the ticker ticks!
You've got to have more margin now; there isn't any doubt.
So you'd better dash with a load of cash
Or we'll have to sell you out!"

That's all I can remember of it, except for a line in one of the verses that went, "And all the little Bears ran downstairs and rang the basement bell!" This little song certainly fit the times. The stock market had crashed the previous October, and the state of the market was on everyone's mind. Of the other songs she taught us, I can remember only fragments. There was the one about "The gay caballero from Rio Janeiro," and "Juanita," which we learned in Spanish. The music taught and sung in most of the schools of the day she tended to ignore. Perhaps it was because we had no songbooks.

A week or so after we arrived at Shoshone, Dad came home from work excited by something new he had seen.

"There are geysers just over the mountain from here," he marveled. "Real geysers like those in Yellowstone Park, but smaller. I saw them today across the valley from the place where we were working."

"When can we go see them?" Rey asked. "Can we go today?"

"No, not today," Dad replied. "They are too far, and we will have to climb up over that mountain there and cross a valley. It's at least seven or eight miles. But I think some of us can go next Sunday."

In the end, Dad decided to take only me. As I was ten, he thought I could make the trip. Rey was disappointed, and a bit resentful. He was sure that if I could make it, he could do it too. But there was no use arguing with Dad. His decisions were final.

Early the next Sunday, Dad and I and one of the section hands named Jim started out. We crossed the highway and climbed to a low pass in the Shoshone Range. From there we could see the geysers across Whirlwind Valley on a white bench at the foot of a range of hills. They seemed to be far away, but we started south down the other side of the Shoshone Range. It was a long way. We didn't get to the geysers until midafternoon. Once we had explored that white bench and watched some of the geysers erupt, it was late in the day. By now I was tired and didn't want to go anywhere, but we still had to cross Whirlwind Valley, which was nothing but a dry alkali flat, and climb back up over the mountain.

"I think we had better not go back the same way," Dad cautioned. "If we are tired now, we will be much more so when we get to the foot of the mountain. We would be risking bad falls trying to find our way in the dark. What we had better do is head for the railroad and follow it on around Shoshone Point."[2]

The first few miles weren't too bad; we only had to walk on the level alkali flat, avoiding the little dirt mounds, each with its clump of greasewood on top. When we got to the tracks sometime after sunset, I wasn't sure I could even climb the embankment. Somehow I did—and then began the worst part of that journey. Every step was an effort, and each time my foot came down, it jolted me clear to the top of my head. All the spring had gone from my legs. I felt like a mechanical toy, putting one foot in front of the other because there was nothing else to do. If we had brought food or water with us, I no longer remember. All I remember is the pain and monotony of that terrible hike along the tracks. Staggering from exhaustion, I made it all the way home on my own two feet. Dad and Jim were not much better off. The trip to the geysers and back had added up to twenty-three miles, and none of us was really ready for it. The next day, Dad and Jim groaned off to work, and I groaned off to school. By the end of the day I felt better, but it took Dad and Jim several days to get the kinks out of their muscles.

By the railroad's standards, the house we lived in was modern; that is, it was supplied with cold running water. The house had four rooms but was really a duplex designed for two families. At times, when no other family needed to share the house, we lived in all four rooms. At the rear of the house, two steps down from the back doors, there was a roofed passageway. Across the passageway opposite the back doors there were a shower and a toilet in separate rooms. There was also a wood-burning monkey stove used to heat water for the shower. The shower and the toilet were intended for use by everyone in the community except the foreman and his family, who had their own facilities.

Water was supplied by a well. A water tank on tall stilts was filled by a gasoline-engine-driven pump. Since the gasoline engine was temperamental and frequently could not be started, the well was also equipped with a hand pump. Two or three of the standard railroad outhouses were still in place, to be used when the toilet couldn't be flushed. When the pump was down, we had to carry water in buckets, as we had been doing since moving to Nevada. It seemed to me that we had to carry water more days than it came through the pipes. At one point, the water tank stood empty for nearly six months. As this tank was not used for watering engines, the railroad was in no hurry to fix it. Finally, by the time a mechanic came to repair the pump, the wooden tank had dried to the point that it would no longer hold water.

9

Men of Influence

From the beginning, Dad and Charlie Helton didn't get along. It was due in part, I think, to Dad's having no patience with people who trifle with the truth.

"Well," Dad said at supper one evening soon after we had arrived, "I guess I am in trouble with my new boss."

"Oh, my! What happened?" Mother asked as she started serving the garbanzos she had cooked with tomato sauce and chorizo.

Dad took a slice of fresh-baked bread and began buttering it for my brother Cyril, who was still too young to do it for himself, and told us what had happened.

"At work this morning Charlie began telling us the trouble his father was having back home in Missouri. The milk snakes had sucked the cows dry. I thought he was joking and started to laugh. But Charlie was serious. He insisted that milk snakes were a problem on many Missouri farms. I told him I had never heard of a milk snake nor had ever seen one. But I have seen snakes, I told him, and snakes can't suck anything because they don't have lips. Well,

Charlie walked off in a huff. He didn't say another thing to me the rest of the day except to give me orders.

"Just before quitting time he said, 'Frank, you ever been to Missouri?'

"I admitted I hadn't. 'Well,' he said, 'I was born and raised there, and I know what I'm talking about. There's all kinds of snakes in Missouri. I know there's milk snakes 'cause I've seen the cows go dry. There's hoop snakes too. They have a horned tail, and they'll take their tail in their mouth and roll down the hill, and anything gets in the way, when that horn hits them they're dead! My daddy's got a dead tree on his place that a hoop snake killed, and I can show it to you.'"

Dad smiled ruefully and shrugged. "Now, how can you argue against logic like that? I'll just have to be more careful about what I say."

Dad tried, but it wasn't easy for him. The foreman just kept piling it on. Charlie Helton had a battery-powered radio, and he would often retell the news stories he heard, adding his own embellishments. One of his stories concerned a test plane that "took off from the ground and flew straight up to over a hundred thousand feet." Dad was incredulous.

"Are you sure about that?" he asked. "Long before it got that high, the engine would have quit due to lack of oxygen, and the pilot would have passed out for the same reason. The plane would have crashed!"

"It's the truth," Charlie insisted. "I heard it on the radio!" What Charlie Helton "heard on the radio" had to be accepted as gospel by the men working for him. Eventually Dad and Mother started playing a little game. Dad would tell Mother what Charlie had "heard on the radio," and Mother would quietly bring up the subject the next time she saw Mrs. Helton. Soon Mother and Dad were laughing over the two or more versions of the same story they were now hearing.

For instance, Charlie began paying attention to the stock market quotations. The economy was looking a little better, and stock prices were going up. He said he was planning to get into the market. In a few days he announced that he had bought one hundred shares of a stock that was really going places. For the next several days he was full of what "his" stock was doing in the market, and how much money he was making.

"Charlie's been following the market all right," Mrs. Helton said after Mother had asked her what she knew about stocks. "He talked about buying one share of this stock that he thought would do pretty well, but the price went up and he didn't have enough money."

One of Charlie's recurring themes was the farm in Missouri where he grew up.

"It's really a plantation: three thousand acres with barns, granaries, and a big white house with pillars in front just like in the pictures! We had horses to ride and mules to work the crops and plenty of hired help. My daddy had four trucks and three cars, and wore one of those white suits when he sat out on the veranda of an afternoon drinking juleps out of a tall, frosty glass."

For some reason he never explained what he was doing in the Nevada desert, working for $125 a month, instead of enjoying all the comforts back home.

In the summer of 1931 he got a telegram urging him to return home as his old daddy wasn't expected to live much longer. He loaded his family into the car and drove off, leaving the section in Dad's care. They were gone about three weeks. The day after they got home, while the men were at work, Mrs. Helton came over to visit Mother and described for Mother her impression of the family plantation.

"The place wasn't all that big," she recounted sadly, "just the yard and the house and maybe ten or fifteen acres. There was old, broken-down farm machinery scattered around. The house had only three rooms, no screens on the windows, and flies everywhere. The old man lay in bed, most of the time in his own dung, 'cause nobody would get him out of bed and onto the pot, and he was too weak to do it by hisself. The flies crawled all over him when nobody was by the bed to wave them away. His daughters, they tried to do what they could, but they also had a bunch of raggedy little kids to do for, and they had to cook for their husbands and the uncles and the nephews who was just settin' around on the broken-down porch. It was sad. It wasn't at all like Charlie said."

"Did you see the tree the hoop snake killed?" Dale asked her. Maybe she didn't hear the question. At least she didn't answer. We went outside to ask Lorraine and Marie if they had seen the dead tree. They didn't know what we were talking about. Apparently they hadn't heard their father's snake stories.

Years later we learned the main reason Dad and Charlie Helton didn't get along. Charlie's stories Dad could laugh off; but it seems that, as a foreman, Charlie was almost totally lacking in the ability to plan his work. As a consequence, the section crew was often doing work that could have been done in a much shorter time or even avoided altogether with just a little forethought. At first Dad tried to offer suggestions to make things a bit easier, but Charlie would have none of it. He merely informed Dad that he, Charlie, was the boss and the gang would do things his way. Dad never mentioned these problems while he was working for Charlie Helton.

George Gale was postmaster at Dunphy. He was also the Western Pacific station agent and telegrapher. As there was no post office at Shoshone, all our mail was delivered to Dunphy. The Heltons didn't send or receive much mail, and they seldom went to the post office; so going to the post office was a task that often fell to Rey and me. It would usually take us a half day to walk the nearly two miles to Dunphy and back because we dawdled. Furthermore, if George, who was a bachelor, took a notion to entertain us, it might take us all day just to mail a letter or pick up a package.

His entertainments were varied. He had a portable phonograph and some records. His tastes ran to what today would be called country and western. Among his collection was one called "Bury Me Out on the Prairie" ("Where the coyotes may howl o'er my grave"). Next to it was "Bury Me Not on the Lone Prairie" ("Where the coyotes howl and the wind blows free"). He liked both sentiments. He also had "Casey Jones" ("Come all you rounders, I want you to hear the story told of a brave engineer") and "The Wreck of the Old 97" ("This is not Thirty Eight, but it's old Ninety Seven. You must put her in Spencer on time"). To round out his collection, he even had a few hobo songs. I remember "Hallelujah, Bum Again" ("Hallelujah, I'm a bum, hallelujah, bum again. Hallelujah, give us a handout to revive us again!") and "The Big Rock Candy Mountain" ("In the Big Rock Candy Mountain, the jails are made of tin. And you can walk right out again as soon as you are in").

He also had two pistols, both revolvers. One was a Colt .45; the other was a five-shot hammerless .38, which he would slip into his pants pocket each time he left the station. He let me shoot the .38 a time or two, but not the .45. He said the recoil would be too much for me. I couldn't hit anything with the .38. The effort to pull the trigger all the way through to turn the cylinder and fire the piece usually put me way off the target. I couldn't even hit a tall stack of old railroad ties from a distance of twenty feet.

George Gale spoke in superlatives. I remember two of his favorite expressions. He claimed that he made a dish of raw beef that was "the best in seven states and four territories." He was also engaged to the "prettiest girl west of the Mississippi." Because she lived in Alaska, up in dogsledding country, he told us he called her "Mush." He made his raw beef dish for us a time or two, and it wasn't bad, but it wasn't exactly raw either. He would get a pot of water boiling on the stove, season it with a number of spices, and drop small pieces of meat into the boiling water. They were left just long enough to be heated through; then we fished them out with long-handled forks and ate them smoking hot.

About once or twice a month the Railway Express Agency would deliver a large box of assorted Hostess Cakes, which he shared with us when we visited. It was such a big box, I often wondered what else he did with all those cakes when Rey and I weren't around. Surely, he didn't eat them all; at least he didn't have the look of a man who lived on pastries.

George Gale wasn't the best of companions for a small boy. He filled my head with a number of things that I wasn't ready for and didn't need. I knew that many of the things he told me would have offended Mother and Dad, so I didn't repeat them. They must have suspected, however, since the last year we lived in Shoshone I was not allowed to visit George alone, and when we went for the mail, we were strictly enjoined to "Hurry home. Don't stay and visit."

About the time we moved from Shoshone in the late summer of 1932, "Mush" came down from Alaska and married George. A year or two later Dad reported that he had been to Dunphy and had seen Mr. and Mrs. George Gale.

"They seem to be doing well," he told us, "and Mush now has a little Mushlet."

Sometime in 1931, Mr. House came to Shoshone. How he arrived, I don't know. He didn't seem to have any transportation of his own, and if he had been riding a train, Shoshone would surely have been an uninviting place to stop. After he arrived, he worked a few days on the section off and on, but most of the time he was unemployed. Whether he was working or not, he continued to live in the east half of our house.

Mr. House was old. At least he seemed to me to be old—much older than Dad. His given name was Rixie; he said he came from Kentucky, and had been a schoolteacher, among other things. He may have taught school at some point, but his impromptu history lessons were refreshing when compared with the history books I read in school.

For instance, as he and I walked over to Dunphy for the mail one cold, gray day, he told me about the Revolutionary War. In colorful terms, he talked about the causes and conditions leading up to the conflict. I don't remember most of what he told me, but I do remember his closing statement as we approached the WP depot that doubled as a post office.

"And so, ol' Jarge Washin'ton took on the British army and whupped the stuffin' out'n 'em. And ever after we've been a free country, and we can thank the Good Lord for that!" He left me wondering if all schoolteachers in Kentucky talked like that.

During the fall and spring when he wasn't working, he spent his days prospecting in the Shoshone Range. He was sure there were minerals there in commercial quantities and was always bringing back rock samples. He may even have prospected the canyon where the Argenta Mine is now operating.

Mr. House had read widely and continued to read everything he could get his hands on. Dad would visit him frequently, and often he would let me go with him. I was fascinated by the things they talked about. I could sit and listen by the hour. I can see them now, discussing an article in a newspaper or comparing the meanings of a word in a dictionary, Mr. House with his head tilted back to read the small print through the bottom part of his glasses, and Dad jabbing the page with his finger. Dad always ended those visits in a relaxed and jovial mood. Talking to Mr. House must have been a considerable relief after spending all day with Charlie Helton.

Not one to waste his time, Mr. House worked on a course in drafting from the International Correspondence Schools when he was cooped up in the house during the winter. Why drafting? He thought it would be a valuable skill to have just in case he decided to become an engineer or an architect.

IO

People Moved In — and Then Moved Out

The year 1931 was an eventful one in our small community of Shoshone; at least it was eventful in the eyes of a small boy who turned eleven that spring. People moved in, stayed a while, and then moved out. Shoshone was so small that any arrival or departure was an event. One or two people even moved in and stayed, and one of these, Blanco, was not even human—he was a dog. Can a dog be considered a person? In my mind he was.

One frosty night I looked out the door opening to the outside from the passageway at the rear of our house and there he was, a white spitz playing with the Heltons' collie. Assuming that he belonged to someone visiting with the Heltons, I watched them for a few moments and then went to bed. The next morning, he was sitting just outside the door. I went out and petted him, and since he looked to me like he was hungry, I went into the house and asked Mother if she had anything I could feed him. She scrounged up a few scraps, which I took out and gave him. He gobbled up everything and then looked around for more.

About that time the Heltons' collie came by. Rey, who had decided we didn't need another dog around, tried to chase the collie home. The spitz, coming to the same conclusion, jumped for the collie's throat. The dogs were snarling and snapping and rolling on the ground, and Rey and I were screaming and scolding and jumping out of the way. Finally, the collie gave up and went home, never to return to that end of the section compound.

As it turned out, the spitz was a stray. There had been no visitors to the Heltons. He just showed up and stayed. Since I had petted him and fed him, he decided he belonged, and from then on would allow no other male dog anywhere near.

Dad said we might as well keep him, at least until someone came to claim him, and from then on he was my particular friend. Except for fighting, he was very well behaved. He was obedient and intelligent, and I was sure he understood every word I said to him.

It was Dad who gave him his name. He named him, he said, for a prominent Mexican army officer he had heard or read about when he lived in Mexico.

"After all," he said, "the dog is white. The name, I think, is appropriate." He was white, all right: the only dark spots were his nose, which was black, and his eyes, which were a dark, dark brown. With his tail curled jauntily over his back, he was handsome.

"Hey, kid," people would occasionally ask, "what's your dog's name?"

Proudly, I would answer, "His name is General Blanco. We call him Blanco for short."

I pronounced the name in the Spanish way, with the *G* in "General" pronounced as an *H,* with the *r* rolled slightly somewhere between an *r* and a *d* sound, and the accent on the final syllable. The *a* in both words was pronounced like the first *a* in "California." Upon hearing the name, most people would give me a strange look. Their expressions clearly said, "What kind of a name is that for a dog?" Mexicans, however, understood the joke, and would smile or chuckle in approval, especially since it came from a towheaded kid who looked as if he wouldn't know a word of Spanish.

The only problem we had with Blanco was that, when he decided to fight another dog, there was just no stopping him. Extremely gentle with children, kittens, and puppies, he always started the fights, and he always lost. He would emerge from a fight with his lips split, his ears shredded, and patches of skin ripped and hanging loose. He just couldn't fight very well. He was old, and his canines—his fighting teeth—were broken off. When he came to us, he was badly scarred from his previous fights. Wearing his scars as badges of honor, he would start a fight with every male dog his size or larger. Usually, within less than a minute, Blanco would be on his back with the other dog chewing at his throat. The hair around his neck, however, was so thick and long that the other dog couldn't hurt him, so he would finally give up. Smaller dogs he just ignored. Or, if they bothered him, he would only growl and move off. I recall one half-grown pup who just wouldn't leave him alone. Finally, at the end of his patience, Blanco flipped the pup over and sat on him.

Sometime in the early spring, Jens came to Shoshone to work on the railroad. Jens (the *J* is pronounced as a *Y* and the name rhymes with "sense") was the eldest son of Mother's Danish friends, the Simonsens. He was probably in his early twenties, and I understood he was engaged to marry a girl in Ogden. The first day he was there he met our schoolteacher, Miss McDonald, and inevitably they began seeing a great deal of each other. Well, maybe not such a great deal, since they were both busy. But they managed to find time.

I may have helped things along. I went with them one Sunday on a short walk to Shoshone Point. There were really no interesting places to walk to, and Shoshone Point was as good as any other destination in that forsaken country. Named for the northern point of the Shoshone Range, Shoshone Point was a very sharp curve where the railroad rounded the mountain range. Just west of the curve there was an overpass where the highway crossed over the SP track. I remember we were resting in the shade under the overpass next to the track. I had climbed up into an embrasure in the concrete framework supporting the overpass, and I could look down on Jens and Miss McDonald.

"Hey," I said to Miss McDonald, "why don't you kiss him?" I didn't think Jens would mind. After all, she had kissed me once, and I hadn't minded it.

After considerable urging, they did kiss, and sure enough, Jens didn't mind it a bit. I don't know if they made a habit of it, though. I did see them kissing one evening when they didn't know I was there. I immediately let them know, abruptly and loudly, what I had seen, and Jens chased me a long way in the dark. For some reason he was very angry. If he had caught me, I would probably have gotten a few bruises.

Was there anything more between them than a few kisses? I didn't think so then, and I don't think so now. Lonely, and attracted to each other as they were, nevertheless they just couldn't afford it. Jens came from a family that held strong views on the importance of chastity in both men and women, and given the mores of the time, any hint of scandal would have destroyed them both, especially Miss McDonald.

When school ended for the year, Miss McDonald went home to Lovelock, and Jens came down with a bellyache. They stopped the midnight train for him, and he went to the SP hospital in San Francisco to have his appendix removed. He went home to Ogden to spend the month required for his complete recovery. While there, he married the girl he was engaged to and never came back to Shoshone.

A few weeks after the Heltons came back from their visit to Missouri, some of Charlie's Missouri relatives came to visit. I don't remember how many there were; I only remember two of them, a niece and a nephew in their late teens or early twenties. I don't even remember their names anymore, so to tell their stories I will have to give them names. The nephew I will call Jim, and the niece Waneeta. Now that I think of it, that may even have been her name, and if it was, she spelled it just like that.

A few days after they came, I saw Lorraine standing outside crying.

"What's the matter?" I asked her.

"It's my cousin, Waneeta," she sobbed. "She's going to have a baby and she's not even married!"

"Gee, how do you know? Did she tell you?"

"No," she said, looking at me, wide-eyed with horror, "SHE'S GOT TITS!"

Of course, we children knew what mothers used to nurse their babies. But beyond that we just never gave it a thought. It hadn't occurred to any of us to conjecture what equipment a young woman, such as Miss McDonald for instance, might have. Even though Miss McDonald had lived with the Heltons for most of a year, she apparently had never exposed herself to the girls. Cousin Waneeta, it seems, lacked the modesty of a Miss McDonald.

Cousin Jim, meanwhile, decided that this was his kind of country. To impress the natives, he sent home to Missouri for his cowboy hat. He must have made a lot of noise about it, because for the next several days, Lorraine and Marie were full of Cousin Jim and his fabulous cowboy hat that was going to come in the mail any day now.

The hat finally arrived. Cousin Jim took it out of the box, put it on his head, carefully adjusted the angle, and, trailed by half the children in the community, strolled across the section compound to the bunkhouse where two or three Mexican gandydancers lived. The section hands were sitting on the step of their little house enjoying the pleasant late afternoon. Jim joined them, and I critically eyed his hat. It had a broad brim like a cowboy hat was supposed to have, but there was something wrong with the crown. It was tall and perfectly rounded and smooth. I was disappointed. It didn't look like a cowboy hat to me.

"Uh, Jim," I asked, when he had gotten comfortably seated on the step, "how come your hat doesn't have a slanty dent in front like the one Tom Mix wears?"

He looked at me for a long moment, and then, his voice dripping with contempt for my ignorance, retorted, "This is the way we wear them in Missouri!"

From his hip pocket he produced a flat bottle, which he passed around to the section hands, each of whom politely took a drink. Taking a pull himself, he began telling tales of the way things were back in Missouri. As he continued to pass his bottle around, he told mule stories, he told wolf stories, and he told outlaw and wild horse stories—each tale a little more fabulous than the one before. He even told snake stories, and I remember he made it a point to tell the one about the hoop snake. I can see him now as he demonstrated with his hands how the snake rolled over and over down the hill, destroying every living thing in its path. The gandydancers who were drinking from his bottle listened politely.

When the bottle was empty, Jim walked over to the fence and threw it into the weeds on the other side of the highway. One of my brothers, either Dale or Grant, full of wonder at the proceedings, went into our house to tell Dad all about it. Dad came out, crossed the highway, searched in the weeds and brought the bottle back. He was disturbed; after all, alcoholic beverages were against the law in 1931. Although Nevada was more or less wide open, people didn't drink in public. They did their drinking in the saloons or in the privacy of their homes.

He walked up to Jim, held out the bottle, and asked, "What was in this bottle?"

Jim bristled. "None of your business what was in that bottle!"

Dad didn't waver. "What were you drinking from this bottle?" He held the bottle out to Jim. After a long moment, Jim heaved himself to his feet. Towering over Dad's five-foot-two-inch height, he snatched the bottle from Dad's hand.

"All right, I'll tell you. There was piss in this bottle!"

Dad just looked up at him. From my angle, Dad looked to be about half Jim's height and less than half his weight. Dad was standing close to him and had to bend his head way back to look him in the eye. Dad shook his head.

"I can't believe," he said mildly, "that a man as big and as smart as you would be drinking piss, especially in front of these children."

His tone suddenly hardened as he went on. "Now we all know—even these children know—what was in that bottle. If you wish to break the law, that is certainly your privilege and your decision. But you will not parade your disregard for the law in front of these children. Two of them are your own cousins! They think you are some sort of a hero! What kind of an example is this to set before them?"

That was the only time I ever heard Dad use that four-letter word. Maybe that is the reason the scene has stayed with me all these years. Although he was a railroad man, and railroad men were noted for their coarse speech, Dad just didn't use that kind of language.

Even today, the scene is clearly etched in my memory. There stood Dad and Cousin Jim with the section hands sitting on the step and the children standing back out of the way. And there stood the railroad houses with their bright yellow paint only a few shades different from the gray-yellow dirt on which they stood. There was the white board fence that surrounded three sides of the section compound and the barbed wire fence next to the dusty highway, the wire stapled to posts made from old railroad ties.

The drinking obviously over since the bottle was now empty, Dad left the scene. Much deflated, Jim tried to recover some of his presence. He swaggered over to the fence and again pitched the empty bottle across the highway.

"Now listen, you kids," he growled, "you just leave that bottle where I threw it, hear?"

That was all right with us. We hadn't touched his bottle and couldn't see any reason why we should. By the time he returned to take his place on the step, the section hands had quietly gone inside to prepare their supper. Through the open door, we could see them beginning to make tortillas and warm up the pot of frijoles they kept on the back of their little four-lidded commissary stove.

It didn't take Cousin Waneeta long to get bored with Shoshone. After all, there was absolutely nothing to do. There were no stores to shop in, and there were no theaters or restaurants to go to; furthermore, there were no young men to make life interesting. Our little community was mighty dull. What was an attractive young girl going to do? In sheer desperation, she decided to Improve Her Mind. There was a young family living in the east half of our house. José García was a handsome man with gleaming white teeth below a trim, black mustache. In the soft summer evenings, when the mosquitoes were not too bad, he would sit on the step of the house where the single men lived and play the guitar and sing some of those plaintive Mexican love songs.

Everyone who was able would drift over to watch and listen and sometimes even join in if the songs were familiar. It was at one of these sessions that it occurred to Waneeta that she really ought to take Spanish lessons, and her teacher would just have to be that good-looking José García. As soon as the entertainment was over, she went to the García home. She had been there a little while, I believe, when I came out of the back door of our half of the house to hear them making final arrangements. Waneeta was standing on the step. The door was open, and I could look into their kitchen and see José and his pretty young wife and his four-year-old son. Neither José nor Waneeta seemed to pay any attention to Mrs. García, who was going about her work as if there was nobody else there but the child.

"That's star wenno, Hosay," Waneeta said as she left with all her arrangements in place. "I'll see yuh mahn-yahna!"

"Star wenno?" I had never heard the term and went in and asked Dad about it.

After thinking about it for a moment, he offered, "She probably thought she was already talking Spanish. She meant to say 'estar,' which means 'to be,' and 'bueno,' which means 'good.' But 'estar,' even if she had used its proper form, is the wrong word to use here. I doubt if José had any idea of what she was trying to say."

"What should she have said?"

"Well, she could have said 'muy bien,' which means 'very well.' However, I very much doubt that she will learn anymore Spanish than she already has. I don't think José's wife, quiet though she is, will allow it, and José is very fond of his wife!"

At the time I was not sure just what Dad was telling me, but his prediction did come true. There were no Spanish lessons. A few days later, Helton's relatives packed their belongings into their ancient touring car and drove off. We never saw them again.

II

Cutting Costs and Other Moves

About the middle of June 1931 Dad learned that he had successfully bid his first permanent job as a section foreman. He was elated. I remember standing in the SP depot in Elko watching in astonishment as he and Mr. House danced and shouted over the news.[1] But the deepening depression was catching up with the railroad, and the job didn't last.

As money began to disappear in markets like New York and Chicago, California growers of fresh fruits and vegetables began cutting back their shipments; to stay solvent, the railroad began looking for ways to cut costs. The number of trains was reduced, of course, but in addition, the railroad started to eliminate sections.

A section was a segment of track, usually seven to nine miles long, the maintenance of which was the responsibility of the section foreman and his crew. As sections were eliminated, the lengths of the sections on both sides were extended to cover the section that had been cut out. When sections were eliminated, the associated dwellings, toolhouses, and other structures were usually moved elsewhere or destroyed, but the way stations where these structures had been located remained for a time. Later, many of the way stations were also eliminated. The side tracks, if there were any, would be torn up and the sign taken down. The next edition of the railroad's timetable would no longer list that station, and train orders would no longer refer to it.

The elimination of sections on the SP's Salt Lake Division began on the division's many miles of branch lines in Nevada and eastern California and then spread to the Joint Operations segment of the main line between Wells and Winnemucca. Under the Joint Operations arrangement, the Southern Pacific track became the westbound track for all trains of the Southern Pacific and the Western Pacific, and the Western Pacific track served as the eastbound track for trains of both roads.[2] Therefore, that segment of SP track was actually a single-track, one-way road; and a section stretching for eighteen miles would have no more main line trackage than a nine-mile section of double track. Sections on double track and the single-track sections with two-way traffic were the last to be eliminated.

Dad's new section was Natchez, located about four miles west of Deeth. The reason he got it, of course, was that no man with greater seniority wanted it. There was nothing attractive about Natchez. The highway, U.S. 40, ran past the section compound just north of the fence. Across the highway, the desert stretched bleakly north to a series of dry hills. South of the tracks, the Humboldt River floodplain consisted of a parched meadow with a line of willows in the distance marking the river channel. Beyond the river were the WP tracks. The terrain then rose abruptly to a low plateau with the Ruby Mountains in the distance.

We all went to Natchez for the Fourth of July. We didn't move everything from Shoshone, because Dad knew that his tenure at Natchez would be short—the railroad had already begun eliminating some of those sections on the branch lines. We took with us just those things we needed for a brief visit. On the third of July, Rey and I had walked the four miles to Deeth and bought a few fireworks, and on the Fourth, in the midst of our celebration, a man we had never seen drove in off the highway.

"I'm Lord," he said.

"I've been expecting you," said Dad, shaking his hand. "You've come to knock me off the Christmas tree!"

I regarded this stranger with considerable hostility. Just who did he think he was, coming here and taking over as if he owned the place? Well, actually he did own the place. He was the new foreman who was bumping Dad. *But,* I thought, *did he have to come in and announce himself as "lord?" Did he think that he had to make a big show and call himself "lord" in order to get respect?* As Dad began introducing him around, I found out that his name was Lord—Andy Lord. He had been foreman of a section on the Modoc Branch that had been cut, and according to the rules, he had to bump the man with the least seniority, who happened to be Dad.

Dad's "permanent" foreman job had lasted just two weeks, and he didn't get another for eight more years. Even after more than sixty years, I look back on that incident with just a tinge of resentment. After all, Andy Lord did take Dad's job.

Sometime during the latter part of the summer, perhaps in mid-July, our little stretch of U.S. 40 that ran past Shoshone became the scene of great activity. The state had begun to turn that gravel road into a hard-surface highway. The contractor was Andy Drumm. He had set up a camp on the north side of the tracks just east of the overpass at Shoshone Point and had started to excavate a gravel pit on the south side of the tracks just west of the overpass. It was a dusty job. They had to build up the grade before paving it, and in doing so they created dust clouds as thick as heavy fog. Just outside the section compound fence, there were piles of yellow dust so thick and loose that when we stepped on them we would sink halfway up to our knees. We thought it fun to wade through the dust in our bare feet.

Mother, however, hated the dust. There was no way to keep it out of the house, or even out of our food. While that project went on, there was grit in everything we ate. That fine dust seeped in even with all the doors and windows closed. But because of the summer heat no one could stand to be inside very long with the house closed up tight. We boys spent most of the time down by the river where we could swim and avoid the dust.

It seemed to us that Andy Drumm's people all drove as if they were in a race. On our way to and from Dunphy to get the mail, one or another of the engineers or supervisors, who drove rattling wood-sided station wagons, would often offer us a ride. They never drove less than fifty miles an hour over that road, construction site and all. The two-and-a-half-ton trucks, which were all they had to move earth with in those days, were also kept moving at top speed.

"It's just the way Andy does business," one of the drivers told me once. "He likes speed, and he likes to get things done in a hurry. When he gets ready to bid on a new job, he starts at one end of the site, and while he drives along he begins to figure the costs in his head. By the time he gets to the other end, he is going maybe sixty miles an hour, and he doesn't stop till he hits Carson City to give 'em his bid!"

It didn't take them long to finish the job. It seemed to me that they graded and paved that section of highway, from a point some miles west of Shoshone to just east of Dunphy, in less than three weeks. And while they were at it, they built a new, straighter approach to the overpass. Not all of the gravel came from the pit west of the overpass. They also began removing gravel from a pit they dug on the floodplain just north of the tracks and next to the east ramp of the overpass. This new pit became important to us the following summer.

In late July or early August, Dad went to Westwood in northeastern California to relieve the foreman, who had decided to take an extended vacation. Dad went by himself, but after finding suitable housing for us (on railroad property, naturally), he sent for us to join him. We packed up all the things we would need, including several bedrolls, boxes of clothing, hand luggage, food, and a crate for Blanco. We couldn't just leave him, so he went as excess baggage, costing us $1.50.

The train we were to take was scheduled to arrive just after midnight. Mother put us all to bed while she did the final packing. Except for Blanco's crate, we had already piled the things to be loaded in the baggage car right by the Shoshone station sign, where the baggage car was supposed to stop. About an hour before the train was to arrive, Mother got us all up. We dressed and had a quick bite to eat. Rey and I put food and fresh water in containers in the crate, carried it out to where our baggage was piled, put Blanco in it, and fastened it shut. We were all out by the side of the track in plenty of time to catch the train.

After waiting out there for a long time in the dark—at least it seemed like a long time—we could hear the train coming, and just as it rounded the curve at Shoshone Point we saw the headlight. It was my job to stop the train. I had a lighted white signal lantern that I was to swing across the right-hand rail. I was supposed to keep this up until the engineer acknowledged with two short blasts of the whistle. But for some reason he didn't answer. I began swinging the lantern in wider and faster arcs. He still didn't acknowledge, and I began to get a little worried. Was he going to run right on past because I was only a kid? But in the dark, how could he tell who was swinging the lantern? About the time I was getting ready to toss the lantern and jump for it, he finally pulled the whistle cord, but by then he was going much too fast. When the train finally came to a stop, the baggage car was three car lengths or more past the signpost where we had stacked our baggage.

Now it was our responsibility to load all that baggage. Carrying their lanterns, the brakeman and the conductor climbed off the train and hurried back to where we were standing and began yelling at us to pick up our stuff, carry it down the track, and throw it into the baggage car. That's where Mother balked.

"Absolutely not! We can't do it. There is just too much. You will have to back the train up!"

"Back the train up?" the conductor shouted. "Lady, do you know what it costs to back up a train like this? We don't back up trains for gandydancers or their families. Now please get moving; we have a schedule to keep!"

Mother stood her ground. "If you want to keep your schedule, you had better back the train. We aren't moving until you do."

"Lady," the conductor growled, "we could just start up the train and leave you here."

"You won't do that," Mother responded calmly. "You won't go off and leave a helpless woman and six children stranded here in the desert in the middle of the night. What would your bosses say if they heard you had done such a thing? Now please get the engineer to back the train."

Outdone, the conductor nodded to the brakeman, who began swinging his lantern in a circle. The train began backing up slowly, and at the brakeman's signal, it stopped with the open door of the baggage car just opposite our pile of belongings. With the help of the brakeman, we quickly loaded our things and then walked back to the first day coach.

Usually shy and unassuming, Mother could be very stubborn when the occasion demanded it. The way the railroad was operating that year, that one train—and only that train—would flag-stop for "deadheads" (that is, stop to pick up passengers riding on passes) one day a week. We would have had to wait a whole week before the train would stop for us again. Mother would not endure that if she could help it.

We detrained at Fernley early in the morning, and then had to wait three or four hours for the branch line train. Blanco was in his crate on a baggage cart and seemed to be all right. He whined to be let out, but we were not allowed to do it.

I don't remember if the branch line train we rode from Fernley to Westwood was a short express/mail/passenger train or a mixed train, nor do I remember how long the trip took. We rode past Pyramid Lake, stopped in

Susanville for what seemed like most of an hour, and then began climbing up into pine-clad mountains. We arrived in Westwood sometime in the afternoon.

Several times during that trip on the branch line, I mulled over an exchange during the night between Mother and the brakeman on the main line train. I had been awake watching the moonlit desert glide by the train window when the brakeman paused by the seat where Mother was sitting.

"I'm sorry for what happened back there," he said quietly. "Know what I think? I think the hog jockey at the head end of this train was asleep."[3]

Perhaps . . . or maybe it just took him a while to remember that that was the day he was supposed to flag-stop for deadheads.

12

Dan

Westwood, California, was the last word in company towns. The whole town—including businesses, homes, schools, church, hospital, and utilities—all belonged to the Red River Lumber Company, which in turn belonged to the Walker family. Dad explained it to me as we were walking from the railroad housing area toward the "company store," the single great building that housed all the business in town. He waved toward the small, unpainted houses lining the street.

"See these houses on both sides of this street? They all belong to T. B. Walker. See that utility pole on the corner? It belongs to T. B. Walker. The store we are going to, and the building it is in, also belong to T. B. Walker. Now, do you see that stick in the road?" He pointed to a split and badly scarred bit of scrap two-by-four at the edge of the unpaved street. "Who do you think owns it?"

"I know," I said, catching on. "It belongs to T. B. Walker!" The fact that Thomas Barlow Walker had been dead for three years didn't detract from the point Dad was making.[1] The Walkers, the children and grandchildren of

T. B. Walker, owned the town absolutely. Although there was a town constable and a justice of the peace, there was no mayor and no council. The Red River Lumber Company never incorporated the town, but instead ran it as the company management (the Walkers) saw fit.[2]

The first morning after we arrived, we were entertained by the strangest-looking contraption we had ever seen on a railroad. It was obviously a steam locomotive—it was on the tracks and was switching cars—but what an odd-looking engine! On the left side it had no big driving wheels, no side rods, no cylinder, and no piston. All the working mechanisms were on the right side. Just ahead of the cab, there were three cylinders with three pistons that operated vertically instead of horizontally. The pistons turned a crankshaft that was coupled to a thick drive shaft that ran from the front axle clear back to the last axle under the tender. The drive shaft turned the axles by means of a beveled gear on the end of each axle outside the wheel.

"It's a Shay," Dad told us. "It's not very fast, but it is supposed to work very well in the mountains. Logging railroads use them."

Somehow, I got the idea that the Shay's ability to climb steep grades was due entirely to the vertical arrangement of the cylinders and pistons—they pulled the cranks up so they just had to provide considerable lift. On the other hand, since the conventional engine's stroke was horizontal, its main propulsive force had to be horizontal and therefore not all that good in the mountains. I had not considered the contribution made by the entire weight of the engine and tender distributed over eight driving axles; nor did I realize that the pistons pushed down as often as they pulled up.

During the first few days after we arrived, we boys—Rey and I especially—explored the area. I don't remember exploring the town, but the surrounding woods and the great pine trees fascinated us. South of town we quickly discovered the Mountain Meadows Reservoir. Although there was a lot of water, it didn't look too inviting for swimming—too many snags and no sandy beaches, just mud. On a high point west of town we could see across Lake Almanor to Lassen Peak, a real live volcano that had erupted only a few years before. I longed to go over there and climb that mountain, but it was forty miles away and too far to walk.

Much too soon after we arrived, it was time for school to begin. I found myself in the sixth grade in a room full of other sixth graders, and it was depressing. I don't recall making any friends during the three or four weeks I attended. The other students weren't hostile, just unfriendly. After all, my father was not a Red River man but an outsider who worked for the railroad, and all his children were therefore outsiders. Grant, however, was having a different problem. A girl named Guadalupe, daughter of a mill worker who lived over in Old Town, thought he was the greatest, but Grant couldn't stand her. We were both glad when we moved back to Shoshone.

The last week in September or the first week in October, Dad's assignment as section foreman at Westwood came to an end. The move back to Shoshone was not without sorrow for me. Dad said we had to leave Blanco behind. Although the cost of the dog's transportation would have been only $1.50, he just wasn't able to spare it. I didn't have any money either, and not because I had spent my allowance—I hadn't had any to spend. I would have loved to have gone to the picture show while we lived in Westwood, but I never had the dime for a ticket. I didn't have a nickel for a candy bar or an ice cream cone either. Although Dad had spent nearly three months working steadily at section foreman's pay, money for us was very scarce. What his financial obligations were at that time, I never knew. So Blanco was placed in the keeping of a young Mexican track laborer who promised to take good care of him until we were able to send for him.

We returned to our half of the house in Shoshone and immediately faced the prospect of school. After their year in parochial school in San Francisco, the Mahoney children were back in school on the Dunphy Ranch. The problem for us was getting there. The Heltons had been driving their children, Lorraine and Marie, to and from school each day, and when we came back to Shoshone they agreed to take my little brothers, Grant and Dale. Rey and I were told that we would have to walk.

Well, it was Saturday, and school could wait until Monday. Rey and I walked over to Dunphy for the mail and to visit our old friend, postmaster and WP station agent George Gale.

"Well," he said, "have you seen Dan Mahoney yet? He's back on the ranch and he's bigger than ever!

"You've got a treat coming," he continued after we admitted that we had never met Dan Mahoney. "The fattest kid west of the Mississippi, and spoiled rotten! He runs his family—his mother, his sisters, and even his poor old dad—as if he were the boss of the range. How he gets away with it, I don't know."

The telegraph sounder, with its Prince Albert tobacco can tucked behind it, began to clatter at that point, and George stopped to take a message.[3]

"One time he went with his dad over to Carlin," he continued after he had written down the message, acknowledged with his own "bug,"[4] and pushed the sounder aside. "This was maybe a couple years ago. Bill Mahoney had business with the owner of one of the stores. Dan, he waits in the front looking at a display of candy in a glass showcase while his dad is talking to the owner in the rear of the store. Dan calls out to Bill and says, 'Dad, I want a candy bar.' 'All right,' Bill says, 'just a minute and I'll get you one.' 'I want it right now!' Dan hollers. 'Just be patient, Dan, I won't be long.' But Dan doesn't wait. He kicks in the showcase and helps himself. Bill pays for the damage, and that's the end of it. Been my kid, he would have got a fair whipping for that one! But nobody lays a hand on him. His mother's afraid he'll get the croup or something and suffocate to death!"

On Monday, a clear frosty morning, Rey and I, dressed in our new riding pants and high-laced boots,[5] walked the two miles to the Dunphy Ranch. The schoolhouse, a one-room affair made from old railroad ties, was situated next to the ice pond, a short distance from the ranch house, and screened by brush and trees. Rey and I cut off from the main road to the ranch and followed a trail along a ditch that led directly to the schoolhouse.

The school was presided over by Miss Catherine Wempe from San Francisco. The fact that she was a devout Catholic and a product of the parochial school system was probably no accident. Bill and Jessie Mahoney had the power to make sure that although their children were not in parochial school, they were at least being taught by a proper Catholic girl. She was a pretty girl with big gray eyes and long, upturned eyelashes that seemed to draw all the cowboys in the area to our school.[6] When she spoke, she also tended to drop most of her final *r*'s. This resulted in some consternation at our Halloween party (which is described in the next chapter).

The students were my brother Dale, who was in first grade; my brother Grant, in third grade; and Marie Helton, in second grade. Lorraine Helton and Teresa Mahoney were in fourth grade, and Rey, Dan Mahoney, and Elsie (an Indian girl whose surname I never learned) were in fifth grade. I was in sixth grade, and Mary and Aileen Mahoney were either in the seventh and eighth grades or in the same grade—probably the seventh since I don't remember anybody graduating that year.

So there was Dan, a year younger than I, a head taller, and outweighing me by a hundred pounds. We became instant friends. Whether or not the stories told about him were true, I don't know. If he was a family tyrant as George Gale made him out to be, I didn't notice. Oh, he would get upset and yell at his sisters, especially at Teresa, but nobody seemed to be too upset about it.

He was no weakling. Once we scuffled in a friendly wrestling bout on the lawn at the rear of the ranch house. *This is going to be easy,* I thought to myself. *A fatty like him is doing all he can just to lug himself around. What can he do?* I soon found out. I easily tripped him, and we fell to the ground, but somehow I ended up on the bottom with about one hundred and eighty pounds of soft, suffocating weight on top of me. I couldn't breathe. I couldn't move. I couldn't even tell him I was giving up. He just lay there on top of me rolling a little from side to side and giggling. Finally, just as I was about to black out, he rolled off. He wasn't agile and he wasn't fast, but he was incredibly strong.

One day shortly after we started school, Rey took me over to an abandoned privy behind the ranch house. Sticking up out of the mess in the pit were the stocks of three or four guns. It seems that Dan, in a fit of spite a year or so earlier, had taken his father's guns and thrown them down the two-holer. No one had thought it worthwhile to get them out.

"I'm going to hook onto those guns with a wire and pull them out," Rey told me. "I've always wanted my own guns, and nobody cares about these."

Although the ranch house was now equipped with indoor plumbing, this privy hadn't been abandoned all that long ago. The stuff holding the guns in upright position was still pretty soft and smelly. I would have liked one of those guns myself, but the prospect of getting one wasn't all that attractive. I told him he was welcome to go ahead, but I wouldn't help.

"I'll help you," Dan volunteered. "I put them there, so I guess I ought to help get them out."

After a little fishing, they managed to hook the trigger guard of a shotgun. Rey heaved the gun up through the hole and dragged it out the door, leaving a smelly brown trail across the blue-painted seat and the neat, gray-painted floor, and on Dan's shoe and sock. Rey dragged it over and tossed into the ice pond, saying that he would let it soak a while before he would begin to clean it up. For some reason he never did get around to cleaning up that shotgun. For all I know, it is still in the bottom of the ice pond, and the other guns are still in the pit where Dan threw them—that is, if the ice pond and the toilet pit are still there.

Each day after school was over, Rey and I were supposed to head for home. Dad had made it very clear that we were expected home within a reasonable time after school ended. However, there were a number of things going on at the ranch that made leaving difficult. It was a temptation to stay and play a while. One day, Rey refused to go. After arguing with him for a while, I gave in and stayed too. We engaged in some fascinating activities, the details of which I can no longer remember, and arrived home at Shoshone after dark. We were well aware of the fate awaiting us. Dad just looked at us and said, "All right, let's go." Neither of us offered any excuses. Anything we said would have been futile.

On the rare occasions when Dad decided he had no choice but to administer corporal punishment, it was always done in private, far enough away from the rest of the community that the resulting noise would not attract attention. We crossed the track and walked down into the meadow on the Humboldt River floodplain. Before we got to the main river channel, we came to an old, dry channel that Dad judged would serve his purpose. He was carrying a couple of solid-looking willow switches. Although it was too dark to see them, I was nervously thinking about them. When we got to the bottom of the channel, he told Rey to go around the bend so as not to witness my punishment. Then he did a strange and most unexpected thing. He threw his arms around me and started to cry. We stood there with our arms around each other and wept. Not a word was said between us. Finally he told me to take Rey's place and send Rey back.

I expected that Rey would get the same treatment I had gotten, but again I was surprised. Rey got a double beating—his and mine. I could hear the blows landing and Rey yelling at the top of his lungs. After a while, they stopped, and we went back to the house. For years afterward, I remembered that episode with guilt. After all, I was the oldest and was responsible. I should have been able to talk Rey into coming home, or failing that, I should have left him and come home alone. But I didn't, and Rey took my well-deserved whipping.

(*left*) Frank Elwood Call, the author's father, in 1917. (*below*) Johanne Calle, the author's mother, enjoying a field of flowers.

The author's sketch of the kind of company house the family lived in in Moor and Shoshone, Nevada. Eight people shared two small rooms in the bright yellow edifice.

Four of the Call children and two small Higleys in front of the famous three-foot tree in Moor, Nevada, 1928. (The tree is still standing.)

The Frank Elwood Call family in Beowawe, Nevada, 1932. *Front, left to right:* Frank Wendell, Rey, Grant, Dale, Adona, and Cyril. *Back:* parents Johanne and Frank, Beowawe, Nevada, 1932.

Adona Call and her friend Florence King in Montello, Nevada, 1936.

Spraying crew exterminating Mormon crickets. 1936. (Courtesy Larry Flowers Collection, The Northeastern Nevada Museum).

Huge piles of Mormon crickets in traps near North Fork, Nevada, 1938. (Courtesy Steve Fargos Collection, The Northeastern Nevada Museum).

The author as a jaunty nineteen-year-old in Montello, Nevada, 1939.

The author's sketch of a railroad foreman's house. "We never got to live in one of these after Dad became foreman, even with our large family."

The author in his World War II navy uniform, 1941.

The author, Frank Wendell Call, in the early 1990s, while he was writing this memoir.

'She's still my sweetheart'

"Sixty years of marriage are remembered with happiness by Mr. and Mrs. Fank Elwood Call as they reflect on other occasions when she wore the same white wedding dress which she made for their Dec. 13, 1916, marriage in the Salt Lake LDS Temple" (*Box Elder News Journal,* December 12, 1976).

After 60 years

Sixty years of marriage haven't taken that special sparkle of love from the eyes of Mr. and Mrs. Frank Elwood Call of Perry, and he's quick to declare "She's still my sweetheart" when asked the secret of their happy married life.

Age hasn't taken its toll on Johanne Call's wedding dress, either, for she's kept it carefully preserved and has worn it for some special events — namely the couple's 50th wedding anniversary open house and a picture-taking session in advance of the family party planned for their 60th anniversary.

She made her wedding dress and trimmed it with inset lace and dainty tatting for the couple's marriage on Dec. 13, 1916, when they were married in the Salt Lake LDS temple by President Joseph Fielding Smith.

This was an especially happy day for Johanne "Yonna" Jorgensen, who had emigrated alone to Utah from her home in Denmark as a girl of 19 in 1911. She was born in Denmark on Oct. 4, 1891.

A Utah Native

Frank Elwood Call was born in Bountiful on Aug. 19, 1892. When he was ten years old his family moved to Mexico, where they lived until 1912. He was the eldest child in a family of 24 children born to his father's two wives.

Four weeks after the couple's marriage, Frank Call was called on a 30-month mission for the LDS Church where he made good use of his Spanish language skills in New Mexico, Texas and Colorado.

This language skill was also very useful in his employment as a track foreman for the Souterhn Pacific railroad, which also meant that the family moved around from location to location along the main line. Their last assignment with the railraod was in Carlin, Nev., and then they retired in 1958 and moved to Perry. He had also been employed with the School for the Deaf in Ogden, returning there between bids on railroad section maintenance.

Active in Church

Through these years of travelling, the Calls and their seven children were active in the LDS Church — always finding a "home" and being involved in the church as soon as they arrived in a location.

Mrs. Call served in the various church auxiliaries through the years, and was a visiting teacher after coming to live in Perry 18 years ago.

He has been counselor to the president of the LDS Branch for the Deaf in Ogden, branch president in Nevada, and stake mission president in the Humboldt LDS stake in Nevada.

Like to Travel

Their life of travel didn't end with retirement. Although she had returned to Denmark for the summer of 1948 to visit with her family, they didn't make the trip as a couple until 1970. Mr. Call had worked at learning the Danish language and says he got lost "on purpose" to see if he could really speak well enough to be understood by the natives.

Four years ago, they purchased a motor home and invited three grandchildren to serve as chauffers on a ten-week winter trip that took them through Mexico and into Guatemala. Last winter, they sought the warmth of Latin America with a plane trip to Yucatan — with both trips finding good use for his Spanish.

He's also delighted in the addition of a granddaughter-in-law from Latin America, and enjoys chatting with her in Spanish while she, in turn, enjoys getting to talk in her native tongue.

Seven Children

These sixty-year sweetheart have raised seven children: Frank Wendell Call of Perry, Rey L. Call of San Jose, Calif.; Grant A. Call, Dale E. Call and Mrs. Eugene (Adona) Nye, all of Ogden; Cyrell Call of Mountain Green, and Lynn B. Call of Los Angeles, Calif.

They are very proud of their 55 grandchildren and 40 great-grandchildren, enjoying pictures of family gatherings and of the youngsters. It is hard to tell who are grandchildren and who aren't, for lots of Perry residents seem to call them "Grandma and Grandpa Call" even if they are not related.

Asked their secret of a long and healthy life, he adds that they do not use tea or coffee, liquor or tobacco; eat very little meat and that is mostly poultry; eat a variety of vegetables and drink lots of carrot juice.

Undoubtedly, part of that secret lies in the peaceful and loving marriage that they've enjoyed through the years and they shared a little smile as he announced that they are still "sweethearts" after sixty years of marriage.

13

Elsie

Elsie, the only Indian student in the Dunphy School, lived with her grandmother in a little house on the ranch and went to school while her grandmother did the Mahoneys' laundry. Elsie was a natural leader. She usually conducted all the games we played during recess and the noon hour. For some reason all the children followed her lead, except perhaps Aileen and Mary, who, being older than the rest of us, thought they were above our childish pastimes.

Without meaning to, Elsie created a sensation during our school Halloween presentation. I don't recall the part she played in the little musical we performed on a tiny stage erected at the front of the schoolroom. The program began just when the evening got dark, and the room was packed. Everyone in the vicinity had been invited, and, as near as I could tell, they had all come. I don't remember what part I played either, except that I was dressed in a two-piece set of yellow silk pajamas that was intended to represent something Oriental. At the end of the play and during the applause that followed,

Miss Wempe put her lips to my ear. "Tell the audience," she whispered, "that there is a chamber of horass outside the school."

"What?" I asked, not understanding. She repeated the words again, and I was totally confused. What is a "horass"? I didn't want to repeat any message I couldn't understand. Exasperated, she went over to Elsie and whispered to her.

Elsie promptly stepped to the front of the stage and delivered the following announcement: "Ladies and gentlemen, for your further entertainment, there is a chamber of whores just outside the school."

The ladies and gentlemen just sat there, astonishment and unbelief written all over their faces. George Gale and the cowboys stampeded for the door.

With great presence of mind, Mary rushed to the front of the stage and shouted, "There has been a mistake! The word is 'horrors.' There will be a chamber of *horrors* outside the school starting in just three minutes!" But by then the cowboys had all gone.

It turned out to be nothing more than an old-fashioned spook alley, with fake cobwebs we had to climb through in the dark, fake monsters to scare us, and fake worms that we had to eat. At least one of the cowboys was disappointed. He still wanted to know where the whores were.

After everyone who dared had been conducted through the "chamber of horrors," we trouped over to the ranch cookhouse for refreshments, and after the doughnuts and cider were all gone, we children went out to enjoy the dark. Elsie as usual took charge. I don't remember now what the game was, but suddenly she ordered Teresa to kiss me. Now Teresa had dark hair, blue eyes, a snub nose, and freckles—and I had this wonderful ache just behind my breastbone every time she looked at me. She was willing, and kissing her was what I wanted to do most, but instead I ran. I was still wearing that silk pajama suit, and I felt especially light and free. She gave chase, but I ran too fast and she couldn't catch me.

In the days that followed, Miss Wempe gradually began to neglect the sixth grade. With several grades in the school, careful scheduling was needed to get through the day, but she wanted to give some of the students a little extra attention. In doing so she often ran out of time. Since I was the only one in the sixth grade and wasn't having any problems with my lessons, she would just say, "Wendell, we will pass up your history class [or geography, or English, or arithmetic] for today. I will hear your lessons tomorrow." But increasingly, on the next day and the days following, I would again be passed over.

At about the same time a terrible thing took place—at least it was terrible for me. The whole school turned against me. It was Elsie's doing, that much was clear, but what I had done to her I never knew. Suddenly I was not welcome to join in any of the games. If I stayed around to watch, the others either left or shouted at me to leave. I don't recall the names they called me. I believe they were mild compared with the words many children use today, but they hurt nevertheless. Were my brothers a part of this? I think they were confused about what was going on and generally not involved. I do remember just once when one of them joined in with the group in pointing out to me what a rotten kid I was. And for what? What had I done?

One bright winter day just a few minutes before the afternoon session was to begin, things got so bad I just ran out of the school. They followed me out, calling me names, but I hid in the snow in a stand of tall sagebrush just to the west of the ice pond. After a while they quit searching and went back into the school. Long after school had started, I got too cold to stay out any longer. I went back in, sat down at my desk, buried my head in my arms, and stayed that way for the rest of the afternoon. I refused to respond to anyone, even the teacher. Even when she ordered me to come up to her desk and pick up a corrected lesson, I didn't go.

Soon the school started to get ready for Christmas. We began practicing for the Christmas program, and things began to relax a bit. I was getting used to being mostly by myself. I don't remember anything about that Christmas program, but I do remember that we drew names to exchange gifts, and the name I drew was—I could scarcely believe it—Teresa Mahoney! I had a total of forty-seven cents, and I pored over the Sears catalog and agonized for days over what I should give her. Finally, with Mother's help, I selected a string of pretty brown beads. They looked like polished stones, but perhaps they weren't real. We exchanged gifts on the last day of school before the holidays. I don't remember what I got or who gave it to me.

Miss Wempe's solution to the problems of the sixth grade was to bring her niece, who was also in the sixth grade, back from San Francisco after the holidays to finish out the school year at the Dunphy School. Miss Wempe explained that now that she had two students in the sixth grade she could no longer neglect it as she had. Her niece was a pretty, friendly girl, and I liked her immediately. The first day of school in January, she stayed with me in the empty schoolhouse during the lunch hour. As we talked, I reminded her that she was missing her lunch, which was being served in the cookhouse. Usually all the children ate lunch in the cookhouse. Those of us who came from Shoshone shared an empty table, where we ate the lunches we brought from home, while the teacher ate with the Mahoney family at a separate table. I had stopped going over to the cookhouse, preferring to eat my lunch alone in the schoolroom, so that day I shared my lunch—homemade bread with peanut butter and honey. She thought it was great, even though there wasn't quite enough for two.

School began to look a little brighter to me. We studied together and competed in a relaxed, friendly way. She was a bright student, and I had to work hard to keep up with her. The hazing I had been getting from the other children became less frequent and eventually stopped—or maybe I simply stopped noticing.

In late January and early February 1932, the big winter storms came. It snowed for days, and the wind piled the snow up in great drifts. The highway, U.S. 40, was closed to all traffic. As a matter of fact, the entire county shut down. Eureka, the county seat, came close to running out of food and fuel. It was seven weeks before the narrow-gauge Eureka-Nevada Railway was able to run a train from Palisade to Eureka.[1] The SP trains still ran on more or less regular schedules, but nothing else moved.

Funds for a school bus to transport the Shoshone children had been made available in late November or early December. The "school bus" was actually an old coupe with a rumble seat. The Helton girls and Dale would sit up front with the driver, an Indian cowboy named Buffalo—that was his last name; I have forgotten his first name—while Rey, Grant, and I rode in the rumble seat. If it was cold, we didn't notice. We had our sheepskin coats and our imitation-leather aviator helmets. We just unsnapped the goggles the helmets came equipped with and turned them down so we could see through the lenses. They didn't really fit very well, and often the cold wind would get under them, bringing tears to our eyes, but we thought they were great. With the highway closed, however, the "school bus" couldn't get through, and we missed nearly three weeks of school.

One bright morning, at about ten o'clock, we heard the jingling of sleigh bells. We rushed outside, and there was our substitute school bus—a big sleigh pulled by a team of horses. Buffalo was driving, but he hadn't come alone. All of the Mahoneys except Bill were on the sleigh, and Miss Wempe, her niece, and Elsie had come, too. The Shoshone children hurried into winter clothing and piled onto the sleigh. Since we didn't get to the school until after noon, it turned out to be a short school day. During the afternoon, a snowplow had cleared one lane of the highway, so we rode home in our regular school bus. The big storms were over. There were no more missed school days due to the weather.

With the coming of warmer weather, the snow melted all along the Humboldt River valley, and the river flooded over its banks. The floodplain between the SP and WP tracks became a series of creeks, ponds, and miniature rivers. Looking at all that water, Rey and I thought it would be a wonderful thing if we had a raft to navigate those streams. There was plenty of material for a raft around the section compound in the shape of old railroad ties, but they were heavy and awkward. The two of us together could carry a tie a few yards, but carrying the ties across the tracks, maneuvering them through the fence, and then carrying them a quarter of a mile to the nearest water was more of a job than we wanted to tackle.

"Let's go over to the place where the road crews camped last summer," Rey suggested. "I bet they left some stuff we could use, and besides, it's right next to the river."

"That's a neat idea," I said. "It's upstream from where we are. All we'd have to do is float it down here to where the river floods over."

So one raw, gray Saturday, we took Dad's hammer and some nails and went over to Andy Drumm's abandoned camp to build our raft.

There wasn't much there. One badly chipped old railroad tie and a few scraps of lumber were all we could find. It would make a skimpy raft, but maybe it would be big enough to hold us. We worked most of the morning by the river's edge, fitting it together, and finally we had a raft. But when we had used up every scrap of wood we could find, it was obvious that it would never hold us both. We had skidded the raft into the river and were holding it against the current with a short piece of rope we had found.

The river was scary. It was in full flood, a brown torrent that actually seemed higher in the middle than near the bank. Now and then little whirlpools would form, twist along in the stream for a few seconds, and then disappear. I hesitated, not sure which one of us ought to try riding the raft. Then Rey let go of the rope.

"Go ahead. I'll see you." He climbed the bank and headed down the river. I should have been suspicious; ordinarily, he would have argued about how he should be the one to take the first ride on the raft since it had been his idea in the first place. Well, it was either get on the raft or let go of the rope and forget it, so I climbed aboard.

It was a horrible ride. The first thing that happened was that the front of the raft got tangled in some brush dragging in the water at the edge of the bank. That awful current caught the back of the raft and pushed it under, and suddenly I was up to my knees in icy water. Then the raft spun around and broke free from the brush. That raft wasn't big enough for even one of us. As the raft spun downstream, I tried to guide it with the makeshift paddle we had fashioned from a split piece of board, but every time I tried to control the raft, it would begin to sink. Finally, after a futile attempt to guide the raft, I had to let go of the paddle to keep from falling into the water. All I could do now was squat down and hang on.

I don't know how long I clung to that wretched raft. All I wanted to do was get off, but there was no place to get off. The banks rose straight up out of the water on both sides. Rey was running along the bank shouting words of advice, but I was too busy trying to keep from being thrown into the water to pay any attention to what he was saying. Finally, the raft swung close to a section of bank that had enough slope that it might be possible to climb out. It was on Rey's side of the river, the side closest to home, and it was less than five yards away. I jumped for it, swam about three strokes, and scrambled to the top of the bank, with Rey helping me the last foot or so.

"Well, there goes our raft," he mourned, looking downstream as it rounded the next bend. "Maybe if we followed it we might be able to guide it into the channel where the river flooded over!"

"And maybe not!" I retorted. "I hope it goes all the way to the Humboldt Sink. I never want to see that stupid raft again. Let's go home. I'm all wet!"

"No, you're not," he said, smirking a little as he looked at my dripping clothes. "Your shirt collar is still dry!" I chased him all the way home, but with my heavy, wet clothes and the water sloshing in my shoes, I couldn't catch him.

For months afterward I had a recurring nightmare. I was on a tiny raft on a raging brown river, riding a current so swift the banks were a blur. Giant whirlpools with gaping, foam-flecked mouths loomed on every side, ready to swallow me up. Just as the raft was being sucked into one of those twisting black holes, I would jump into the water in a desperate effort to swim to the bank, and at that point I would wake up.

Elsie left the school and the ranch before the end of the term. The snow was gone, mud was everywhere, and green was beginning to show around the roots of last year's clumps of grass still standing in the meadows. I came back early from lunch in the cookhouse one afternoon and found Miss Wempe sitting at her desk crying. She had apparently been there all during lunch. She gave no sign that she had noticed me, and I quietly eased back out the door. I had never seen a teacher cry, and it hurt to watch her.

By the time school was ready to begin, she had stopped crying, but she looked very sad. I asked her niece if she knew what the matter was, but she just shook her head. Neither Dan nor Elsie was in school that afternoon, and Elsie and her grandmother left the ranch that same day. Dan was back in school the next day, and no one ever talked about it. I never saw Elsie again.

One Sunday toward the end of the school year, the Mahoneys stopped at Shoshone on their way to attend mass in Battle Mountain. Mrs. Mahoney gave Mother a box of odds and ends, telling her that they were things her children no longer wanted, and perhaps the Call children could find some use for them. One item in that box I will always remember; it was the necklace of pretty brown stones I had given to Teresa for Christmas. It gave me a strange, rather lost feeling to see it there, but I pretended I had never seen it before. My sister Adona played with it for a few days, and then it disappeared. Nobody missed it.

14

Death of a Way Station

The 1931–32 school year ended the first week of May. Miss Wempe and her niece went back to San Francisco, and the Call children began enjoying the summer. Swimming was of course the main order of the day, but we had to find a new swimming hole. The river, true to form, had adjusted all its channels and had filled up our old swimming hole with gravel; the water was only a foot deep. During the spring floods, however, the overflowing river had filled the gravel pit that Andy Drumm's road crews had dug the summer before just west of the new approach to the overpass on the north side of the tracks. It was big, deep, and easy to get to—a short walk east along the tracks. The water was muddy at first, but later it cleared, and we could see the bottom in most places.

One Saturday after work Dad went with us. After we had been swimming a while and were resting on the bank, he turned to me and said, "You're a good swimmer. How far do you think you can swim?"

"I don't know," I answered. "I just never thought about it."

"Do you think you can swim around this pond?"

"I can try," I replied, and I started to get up.

"Wait," he said. "You're tired now. We'll come back tomorrow morning when you've rested, and you can give it a try."

The next day, we were all assembled on the edge of the gravel pit just below the railroad embankment. We were all there except for Mother, Adona, and Cyril, who had stayed home. "Stay close to the bank," Dad advised me. "There may be no one to help you if you should get into trouble."

I slipped into the water and started to swim slowly, taking my time. I stayed close to the banks, which were steep and where the water was deepest, except for one corner closest to the slope of the overpass where it was very shallow. I swam as far up into that corner as I could without touching the bottom. After one circuit, I didn't feel tired, so I kept on swimming. After the second time around, I thought I could do it again. At the end of the third trip, I had had enough. I didn't exactly need help to get out of the water, but it was close.

Dad then paced off the distance around the pond, and after some figuring to allow for the shorter distance I had taken inside his measurements, he announced the result.

"Six thousand feet, or a little more. That's more than a mile!" Everyone applauded, and, tired as I was, I felt pretty good. After that bad school year, it was nice to know I was good for something.

During the summer, the railroad's problems with the depression became increasingly evident. Train crews began setting out surplus Pacific Fruit Express cars on any convenient side track for storage. Almost every station with a little-used side track was put to use, and there were hundreds of cars to store. The cars were spotted in sets of five coupled together, with a space of a car length or two between sets.[1] The side track at Shoshone got its share. A day or two after the cars were set out, we discovered that it was great sport on our way home from swimming or the post office to climb to the top of the first car, walk along the catwalks on top of the set, climb down, and go on to the next set and repeat the process until we got tired of climbing. The first car of one of the sets, however, had water dripping from the drain under the ice bunker at one end of the car. When we had climbed to the top of the car, we opened the cover to the ice bunker, and, sure enough, there were several hundred pounds of ice that had still not melted. We didn't need ice. There was plenty of ice in the icehouse at Shoshone. But what intrigued us was the strong smell of bananas.

We climbed down and went to the main door of the car. It was sealed with a metal seal and a red tag. We broke the seal, climbed into the car, and, to our delight, found bananas scattered all over the floor. Most of them were green, but there was also a big pile of overripe ones near the door, the source of the aroma we had noticed. Overjoyed by our discovery, we ran home, got some bushel baskets, went back, and gathered up every ripe and green banana we could find. Some of them had slipped down between the floorboards. Those boards were braced a few inches above the main floor of the car to allow the cool air from the ice bunkers to circulate. We raised the boards and salvaged every last usable banana, nearly two and a half bushels in all.

Proudly we carried them home. For once in our lives we were going to have all the bananas we wanted. We were going to gorge on bananas. We might even get sick on bananas. When we showed Mother what we had found, her eyes lit up with pleasure. But then her thrifty European upbringing took over.

"You may each have one banana. Then you must put the rest down in the cellar. You may each have one banana every day until they are gone." There was no use arguing; we did as we were told, regretting that we hadn't eaten two or three bananas while we were still in the PFE car.

It became obvious in a day or two that some of the green bananas would not last long enough to ripen. Mother brought them into the house and cooked them. That was the only time I ever ate fried green bananas.

We started systematically to open every car on the side track to see what else we could find. There were no more bananas, but we found a half bushel of potatoes, eight or ten pomegranates, and half a flour sack of raw peanuts. Then we had to stop. One of the railroad officials, in passing through, noticed that the seals were gone from some of the cars, and an order came down the line that we were to stop opening cars. Well, we didn't exactly stop; we just went around to the other side of the cars, away from the main line tracks. Because of the slope of the embankment, the doors were nearly out of our reach, but we managed to open some of them and climb in anyway. We didn't find anything interesting, though.

In July, the railroad eliminated the Shoshone section, an action that drastically changed the lives of some in our tiny community. The Heltons were the hardest hit. Charlie Helton was apparently on the bottom of the seniority list, and there was no one he could bump. He did have a business he could fall back on, however. He owned a service station.

During the previous autumn, he had started talking about how Shoshone would be an ideal place to sell gas.

"Look here," he would say to anyone who would listen, "it's at least twenty-five miles either way you go to the next gas stop. It's either Battle Mountain or Primeaux's at the top of Emigrant Pass. The road is paved now, and traffic is bound to pick up. I could sell a lot of gas here."

He spent some time tramping through the sagebrush on the south side of U.S. 40, then announced that he had located a Geodetic Survey section marker, and from that he located the spot where he intended to build. Later he announced that he had title to the property, but it was unclear to me whether it was railroad property or public land.[2]

During the winter he spent his spare time building his station out of old railroad ties, which were available just for the taking. After some urging from Charlie, Dad agreed to dig a well on the property at the rate of a dollar a foot, to replace a dry well already there. He and Mr. House worked on the well during the winter, digging it by hand on Sundays. At about forty-five feet, with not a sign of water, they ran into trouble. Sand began flowing in from the sides as fast as they could shovel it into the hoist bucket and haul it out. Dad tried to stem the flow by making a casing of railroad ties, but it didn't work. The sand continued to flow, and they had to quit.

"Not one dime," Charlie said. "I'm not payin' one dime for a dry hole!"

"I didn't guarantee to find water," Dad rejoined. "I just contracted to dig a hole down to the level of the existing well, and that's where it is now."

"I don't give a damn if you went all the way to China. That there's a dry hole, and I'm not payin' for it!"

So effort on the well was abandoned, and Charlie continued to build and furbish his service station. It was Texaco, if I remember correctly, that installed the tanks and pumps.[3]

One day shortly after the river rose and flooded over its banks, someone noticed that there was ten feet of water in the new well. Charlie came over and paid up.

"Here," he said, placing the bills in Dad's hand. "I tol' you all along I'd pay you forty-five dollars for the well!"

The Helton family operated the service station during the spring and most of the summer, until Charlie lost his job. The service station hadn't brought in all that much revenue. It was too new, and the traveling public didn't know it was there, as none of the road maps showed its existence. Charlie decided to pack up and move, and he sold the station to Mr. House, who thought he could wait it out until business improved. "It's bound to get better," he reasoned.

One hot summer day, the Heltons packed up their car, loaded in their children and their dog, and headed east. I got the impression they were going to Eureka, but I don't know for sure where they went. Except for Mr. House and the Calls, Shoshone was now empty. All the section hands except Dad had gone. The railroad kept Dad there for a few weeks to act as caretaker until they could demolish or remove the buildings. His new boss was Felipe Gonzales, foreman of the Beowawe section. In late August, the railroad told us to leave, and Mr. House remained as the only resident of Shoshone.

It took several years for Shoshone to die. Within a few months, the buildings were demolished or moved elsewhere. The stored PFE cars were eventually removed; then the side track was torn up, the sign was taken down, and the railroad no longer had a station called Shoshone. Mr. House, meanwhile, expanded his services to include cabins for rent, single-room affairs made from old railroad ties, offering the absolute minimum in accommodations. Road maps of Nevada began referring to it as "Rixie's Place" or "Rixie's Camp."

I never saw Mr. House again. Sometime after we left, I heard that he had died. Then for a number of years his daughter operated the place. I stopped there a time or two and visited her briefly when I was passing through. Eventually, she too died, and Rixie's began to disappear a little at a time. The cabins and the original service station sat empty for a while, with one of those old hand-operated gas pumps facing the old highway. A new version of U.S. 40 had been built south of the old road, which put it to the rear of the original station. (There was plenty of empty country there. Instead of reworking the old road, the highway crews just moved over and built a new one.) Then the new I-80 was built still farther south, with Exit 254 at the spot where Shoshone used to be, and the interchange was named Dunphy. A new service station was built, equipped with electric lights and other modern conveniences, and then it too died.

Sitting on my desk as I write this is a flat rock, a pebble from the riverbed. It is about three and a half inches across and a little more than half an inch thick. On one side someone has painted a red, yellow, and green turtle with the legend RIXIE'S CAMP, NEVADA, and the words U.S. 40 in silver paint. On the other side is a map of the state of Nevada, with the words TRAVEL U.S. 40. SHORTEST SAFEST FASTEST THROUGH NEVADA. It had lain on a windowsill in Dad's house for a number of years after his retirement. Who did the artwork on the rock? Was it Mr. House, or his daughter? And when was it done? I will never know.

15

Beowawe

At the end of August 1932, we moved to Beowawe. It wasn't a long move, only about eight miles by rail and still in Eureka County. The town is today situated six miles south of the Beowawe Interchange, Exit 261 of I-80. In 1932 there was no interstate highway. A dirt road led from U.S. 40 to the town, which consisted of about a hundred people. There was a two-room schoolhouse, two general stores, two saloons, and no church. (I was under the impression in those days that a Nevada town had to have at least three saloons before it was big enough to have one church.) Most of the inhabitants of the town worked for one of the two railroads, the Southern Pacific or the Western Pacific.

Our new home was a three-room house in the center of town between the SP and WP tracks. It had a kitchen, a living room, and a bedroom. The living room was long and narrow; obviously it had been converted from an old boxcar. Mother and Dad curtained off one end for their bedroom.

The railroads split the town in two, and ours was the only dwelling between the tracks. We soon found out that we were in the middle in more ways than one. Most of the people living on the south side of the tracks hated those living on the north side, and those on the north side reciprocated.

The trouble had apparently started between the proprietors of the two rival general stores in town. Jack Tyler had the store on the south side of the tracks, and Andy Allen had the store on the north side. It was expected that each family in town would be loyal to its "own" store. As we were literally in the middle, Mother and Dad decided to join neither group. It wasn't really difficult, since they did not depend on either store for groceries and other necessities, preferring to have these things shipped out from Ogden.

As there were no stores in the places we had lived in up to then (except for Westwood), we were able to have our supplies shipped by rail "free billing," that is, with the railroad picking up the cost. But in Beowawe, with two stores available, the railroad decreed that we would either buy locally or pay the freight. Yet with the high local prices, Mother and Dad found it was still cheaper for them to buy in Ogden and pay the freight. This arrangement wasn't popular with either of the storekeepers, but it enabled the Call family to treat both factions, north and south, evenhandedly. If the squabble between the north and the south ever carried over to the children in town, we didn't notice.

It didn't take long for us to get established in Beowawe. Our friendship with the Gonzales family was immediate. Felipe Gonzales was the foreman of the Beowawe section and therefore Dad's boss when Dad was not relieving a foreman somewhere on the line. The Gonzales children were Brigido ("Brig"), who was considerably older than the rest of us and was gone most of the time; Benito ("Ben"), who was about my age or a bit younger; José ("Joe"), who would have been about Grant's age; Lauvro ("Lavarr"), about the same age as Dale; Evangelina ("Vangie"), the same age as Adona; María, perhaps two years younger; and Alejandro ("Cando"), about two years old.

The foreman's house where the Gonzales family lived was close, just across the SP tracks from our house, so we spent a great deal of time there. Felipe was a pleasant, soft-spoken man. He had a large black mustache and a quiet way of speaking to his children that commanded instant attention and obedience. His wife was young looking and very pretty. She had lovely ivory skin; in contrast, Felipe's complexion was a dark mahogany. Their children's complexions fell somewhere in between.

The last member to make up the household was Felipe's mother, whom we all called "Abuelita" (Little Grandmother). She had her own room with a little shrine where she spent a great deal of time praying. Often when we visited the Gonzales children, the door to her bedroom would be open, and we would hear her quietly murmuring her prayers as she held her beads.

The other family with whom we had the most to do was the Sansinenas. They lived in a little house perhaps a quarter of a mile south and east from the Gonzales home. The house had a high, wooden false front, indicating that it had once been used as a store. I don't remember much about Mr. and Mrs. Sansinena. The oldest of their children was Paul, who was perhaps two years older than I. Leon, their second son, had graduated from the eighth grade the previous spring and was attending high school in Eureka. Their daughter Emily was about Rey's age. There may have been younger children, but I don't remember them.

Beowawe (Bee-oh-WAH-wee). A strange name. An Indian name, we were told, but what did it mean? Dad said he had been told it meant "Big Gate."

"See that hill right there at the edge of town? And do you see that hill over there to the north? The river, the railroads, and the town are squeezed between those two hills. They make a big gate."

The Indian children who lived with their families a short distance away to the south of the town had another definition. When asked, they would turn around, point to their rears, and say "big." And that was all. They would repeat "big" and point. They were literate and spoke English well enough, but for some reason they never spoke the English word for what they were pointing to.

Many years later I ran across a book in the Carnegie Library in Ogden written by a man who had been the superintendent of the SP's Salt Lake Division. In his version of how the Central Pacific had built the railroad through the area, he told about a man whose job it was to give names to the stations as the railroad progressed.

It seems that one day as he was riding his horse along the proposed right-of-way, he had an urgent call of nature. Looking around, and apparently being alone, he dismounted, undid his belt, and squatted down to take care of it. Now he was a fat man with a considerable spread across the hips. Suddenly he heard laughter behind him. In consternation, he looked around. And there was a group of Indians—laughing, pointing to the pale full moon he was displaying, and shouting, "Beowawe! Beowawe!" The next town he named, he called Beowawe. I don't remember the title of the book or the name of the author. It is no longer on the shelves of the library in Ogden. I am still looking for it.

The 1932–33 school year in Beowawe started the day after Labor Day. Beowawe had a two-room schoolhouse with a bell tower over the front entrance and a bell that was rung each morning before school. The first room, just behind the front entry, was presided over by Mrs. Ethel B. Carter, who taught the first through fourth grades and was also responsible for ringing the bell. In the second room at the rear of the building, Mrs. Myrtle I. Wright taught the fifth through eighth grades. In addition to teaching, she was also the principal. At a respectable distance from the rear entrance were two privies, one for the girls and one for the boys.

My sister Adona started school that year. She and Vangie Gonzales were in first grade. I don't remember all the children in the school. I don't even remember all those in the upper-grades room. But I do remember a few of them. There were Benito and José Gonzales, Virginia and Robert E. Lee, Emily Sansinena, June Williams, Harold Lamb, Joe Andreozzi (Junior), Ircel Carter (Mrs. Carter's oldest son), and Aven Buffalo. My brother Rey was in sixth grade, so both of us were in the upper room. Grant and Dale were with Adona in the lower room.

Aven Buffalo, a brother of the Dunphy school bus driver, was one of the Indian students. The Indian population of Beowawe was represented by the Buffalo family, the Dick family, and the Dann family, among others. So in the school there was a Dick Dann, a Dan Dick, and several Buffalos. The Indian children received clothing grants. On the first day of school each of the boys would show up wearing stiff, brand-new Levi's. Even the first graders had them. I hadn't known that Levi's came in such small sizes!

Mrs. Wright had a strange way of teaching. Most of what we learned that year we learned by rote and by constant repetition. She held a series of contests to which she invited parents and citizens of the town, and she drilled us exhaustively to get ready for them. They covered all the subjects taught, and during any contest she never asked a question that we had not previously been drilled on. Those who missed a question sat down. When she ran out of questions, those still standing were declared winners. The only real competition was in the math events, in which the first one to solve a problem was the winner. Although I was required to participate in the math events, I never won one of those. I was in the winners' line in all of the other events, though. Winning didn't seem like much of an accomplishment since there were so many in each line. How I used to wish she would just once have a real spelling bee that would continue until one student was a clear winner!

One day during the first week, she sent the seventh grade (there were four or perhaps five of us) to the board. "Write this sentence on the board," she directed us. "Now, diagram the sentence."

While the rest of the class were busy making funny little lines and writing words on them, I just stood there.

"What's the problem, Wendell? Don't you know how to diagram a sentence?"

Puzzled and embarrassed, I finally choked out, "No, Mrs. Wright, I don't know what that means."

"Well! How do you expect to ever learn the parts of speech without knowing how to diagram a sentence?"

"Oh," I brightened, "parts of speech!" I then turned back to the board and began to write above each word the part it represented in the sentence.

Mrs. Wright grumped a little, and then said, "Well, you have them all right, but I don't see how you can do that without first diagramming the sentence." That was the last I heard about diagramming. I still can't diagram a sentence. I have thought since that Mrs. Wright could have used a copy of Miss McDonald's fifth grade workbook.

She was good, however, in directing dramatic and musical presentations, most of which she cleverly adapted to fit our town and the children she had to work with. I was frequently paired with June Williams in short skits or musical numbers, some of them in blackface, which was very popular. We presented several of these during the winter at our biweekly community parties, which are described in Chapter 17.

16

The Year We Got Nothing for Christmas

I shall never forget Christmas 1932. I was twelve years old that year, and we were in the third year of the Great Depression. Herbert Hoover was completing his last year as president of the United States. Franklin D. Roosevelt had been elected president in November and was waiting to take over in March 1933. And 1932 was the year we got nothing for Christmas.

Those were tough times. The rich farms and orchards in California had almost stopped shipping fruit since there was very little money in Chicago and New York to buy it. Because of reduced freight traffic, the railroad, to stay in business, had to reduce costs; and the railroad's first reductions always seemed to come out of the Maintenance of Way Department where Dad worked. That year, instead of laying off workers, the SP chose to keep a full crew, but work each man only three days a week. At three dollars a day, Dad's income amounted to only nine dollars a week with which to maintain a family of eight. Nine dollars a week—even with house, lights, and fuel thrown in—was not going to provide much in the way of Christmas.

With considerable ingenuity, Mother had managed to scrape enough money together to buy each of us a pair of new shoes. This was to be our Christmas. However, she was faced with a dilemma. A Christmas program was to be given at the Beowawe school on Friday just before Christmas, and all her children except Cyril were to participate.

Mother couldn't stand the thought of her children appearing before the entire town in our broken, worn-out shoes. If she gave us our new shoes on Friday, there would be nothing for Christmas morning. Resolutely, she decided that the Friday Christmas program was more important, so just before we went over to the school, she gave us each a box containing a new pair of shoes.

On Christmas morning there was nothing under the tree. There wasn't even a tree. Evergreen trees didn't grow in that part of Nevada, and we had a tree only when we could cut one ourselves. My youngest brother, Cyril, who was four that year, did get a present—Dad's beloved harmonica. Mother insisted that he was just too young to understand and cope with the disappointment.

But wait! What about Grandma's package? She always sent a package at Christmas every year with something for each of us. How she managed to do this I never understood. At that time she had more than fifty grandchildren, and her means were limited. Were we the only grandchildren she sent presents to? To this day, I don't know.

But Mother said, "No. There is nothing in Grandma's package for any of you this year. She just couldn't afford it."

Well, hoping against hope, we watched as she opened the precious package, and all there was in it was a patchwork quilt. Not even a whole quilt—just the top shell. Disappointment was sharp for a little while, and I noticed a few quiet tears on some faces. Mostly though, we were all trying hard not to show our feelings. Cyril, meanwhile, was cheerfully playing his harmonica.

Perhaps we mourned for all of ten minutes. It couldn't have been much more than that. I realize now that Dad and Mother were much more disappointed than we children were, and that their grieving must have lasted much longer. But there were important things to be done—breakfast, for instance—and we got busy.

Breakfast on that Christmas was like breakfast on every other morning that winter—cooked cereal, either oatmeal or cracked wheat. The raw cereal was placed in water in the pot the evening before and allowed to soak on the back of the wood stove all night. When cooked, it was served with condensed milk and sugar. If we complained about the monotonous diet, Mother invariably told us about the time when Dad was a little boy. Sugar was so scarce that the children were allowed to have a little sugar only with their third bowl of cereal. The first two had to be eaten without.

After breakfast we went over to see what the Gonzales children had gotten for Christmas. They had a lot of new things that they were perfectly willing to share with us while we visited. Felipe Gonzales, Dad's foreman, was working six full days a week and therefore received his full salary. With house, lights, and fuel free, foremen were very well-off.

Christmas afternoon was a time for visiting and receiving visitors. Our home was a popular place, not only for children but for the adults in town as well. Poor as we were in material things, Dad's warm, outgoing nature and Mother's superb Danish cookies and cakes seemed to attract visitors from all around town. Even the Williamses from the emergency airport a mile or two west of town came to visit, and they brought their daughter June, who I thought was the most beautiful girl in the whole world.

In the early evening we had a taffy pull. Soon after arriving in any new house, Dad would drive a huge nail into the trim at the side of the kitchen door. This nail was not to be used as a coat hanger or anything else, but only for pulling taffy. Our friends, the Gonzales children and the Sansinena children and others, loved to come over to our house for a taffy pull.

A mixture of sugar, water, salt, and a little vinegar was boiled on top of the kitchen stove until a small sample cracked when dropped in a glass of cold water. It was then spread out on the tabletop to cool. While it was still too hot to handle comfortably, Dad coated his hands with butter—or probably margarine, since it cost only ten cents a pound and butter cost at least twice as much. He then gingerly gathered up the mass and threw it up over the nail, which previously had been coated with butter, along with the surrounding door trim.

As it sagged from the nail, he put a little more butter on his hands, and when it looked as if the whole thing was about to fall to the floor, he flipped it up over the nail again. He continued to do this until it had cooled enough that he had to pull it to stretch it. As it cooled, and as he continued to flip it over the nail and stretch it, the taffy gradually turned snowy white and took on a beautiful shiny luster.

Each of the children present had gotten a small portion to pull in our hands. The taffy we were pulling for some reason never acquired this luster, taking on a patina of a different hue—due perhaps to hands that were not very clean.

When Dad judged the consistency right, he removed the taffy from the nail and stretched it in long ropes on the table, handling it carefully so as not to pinch it and close up the pores. He then cracked it into small pieces with the back of a table knife. A perfect piece of taffy was one that had many small holes through it, was brittle enough to break when struck with the back of a knife, but tended to go a bit chewy in your mouth. Delightful! I can still taste it!

With plenty of taffy on hand we then gathered around a potbellied heating stove in which the fire had been built up until the sides glowed red, and Mother told us stories of Christmases in other times and other places. Her favorites were from Hans Christian Andersen, and she told us about "The Little Fir Tree," "The Little Match Girl," and "The Snow Queen." She was a marvelous storyteller. When she told a story, the characters lived and moved across the stage of our imaginations, and we could never get enough of them. We and our friends loved to hear them over and over again.

Much too soon it was time for the other children to go home, and we all went out into the frosty night. Our visitors had to wait a few minutes for a mile-long, westbound freight train to rumble past our house before they could cross over the tracks. As the caboose rolled by at nearly sixty-five miles an hour, we waved and shouted "Merry Christmas!" to a trainman standing on the lowest caboose step. We could see a flash of white teeth in a shadowed face as he smiled and waved back, and then was gone.

As we children grew older, we used to think of that time as the year we got nothing for Christmas. But did we really get nothing? It took us a few years to realize that the best part of Christmas is not necessarily the gift you can hold in your hands.

17

"But What Did You Do for Entertainment?"

Entertainment was not a word often heard in tiny-town Nevada in the late 1920s and early 1930s. People didn't think they needed to be entertained. So what did they do in their leisure time in those remote railroad way stations?

If they had transportation, they could drive to the nearest town—Wells or Elko or Winnemucca, for instance. They could go to a dance, see a movie, or go to a saloon to drink or gamble. For those who didn't have transportation, or chose to stay at home, there were few choices. They could read. Most people did read, and they read whatever they could get their hands on. What a dreary existence it must have been for those few who didn't know how to read! Books were scarce, but magazines were delivered regularly to those who subscribed to them, and newspapers were quite plentiful. Although many families subscribed to newspapers, it generally wasn't necessary to do so to keep up with current events. Newspapers were dropped off by train crews several times a week.

Many travelers, when leaving a train at Ogden, for instance, would leave the papers they had purchased on the train seat. The train crews would gather them up, put an elastic band or a string around each one, and drop them off at isolated stations along the line. Carlin was the division point for passenger train crews. Thus, east of Carlin the *Denver Post* was a familiar friend, while west of Carlin the *San Francisco Examiner* was a frequent delivery. Although I never heard anyone express it aloud, the general feeling of those living alongside the railroad tracks was *God bless those thoughtful trainmen!*

Those who had radios were truly fortunate. Radios were expensive, cumbersome affairs that were powered by a car battery and an array of No. 6 dry cells.[1] Radios were scarce. Jess Higley in Moor had one, and it may have been the only one in the community. Charlie Helton in Shoshone had a radio, and of the several sets in Beowawe, the Gonzales family had one. As a rule, people didn't spend much time listening to the radio. Batteries were expensive and short-lived, and programs were chosen with care. Families would gather around their radios for those selected programs, and when they were over the radios were turned off.

Telling stories and reading aloud were two of the pleasures we enjoyed as children. Odell Higley was a fabulous storyteller who made up stories as he went along. Often he would begin a story and tell it in chapters on successive evenings. His themes were usually western. Odell, Blain, and I would lie in the dark in the same bed, and Odell, usually after considerable urging from Blain and me, would begin a story. From these stories, I developed a love for western literature that has stayed with me to this day. Did Odell go on to become a writer? No, he became a jockey, and as far as I know he never wrote a single story.

Mother was also a great storyteller, and she had a ready fund of children's stories that she would tell on almost any occasion. They became so familiar that if she deviated from them in any way the children would correct her. Each story had to be told the same way each time. Seated in a comfortable chair, with the children gathered around her on the floor, she would become, in turn, each of the characters of her story. She never gestured with her hands. A slight movement of her head and a change in her voice and the way she talked did it all. To this day in my mind I can see the old witch with the crooked back and the gravelly voice enticing the chubby boy, Fatty Lamb, into her sack so she could throw him over her shoulder and carry him home to become the main ingredient of the soup she planned to serve to her witch guests and the witch girl.[2]

Winter evenings were often spent gathered around the kitchen table listening to Dad or Mother read aloud from books they owned or had managed to borrow. The only light would be a kerosene lamp in the middle of the table. The rest of the room would be in deep shadow. A roaring fire in the kitchen range kept the room warm and cozy.

As we grew older and became better readers, we children were permitted to take our turn at reading aloud. Always there were sighs of disappointment when Mother or Dad would say, "That's enough; it's time for bed! We will continue the story tomorrow." There was also a sigh when a beloved book ended. I can remember our entire family sitting in the warm kitchen in Shoshone and laughing over the antics of two wacky ladies who were ambulance drivers in the Great War. As I recall, their adventures were recorded in two books entitled *Tish* and *More Tish.*

At Moor one winter, Dad and Mother instituted a weekly "home evening." The purpose was entertainment. We played games, sang songs, and performed "shadow plays." For a shadow play, a sheet was strung across the room. The audience sat on one side of the sheet with the actors on the other side. A row of kerosene lamps against the wall cast shadows of the actors against the sheet.

With our parents' permission, we began to invite the Higley children over for home evening. The Higley children soon invited their parents, who then invited others in town, until we had a community home evening. With the approach of spring, and longer days, the home evening gradually disappeared.

Dad and Mother were also largely responsible for a series of community entertainments in Beowawe. These community get-togethers grew out of an effort to bring religion to the town. There was no church in Beowawe. About twice a year an itinerant minister, the Reverend Schriver, would visit the town and hold a worship service.[3] But twice-yearly services were not enough. To fill the void, several families got together and organized a nondenominational community Sunday school, which met each week in the town hall.

The Sunday school was organized with a superintendent, an organist, a music director, and Sunday school teachers. Then someone suggested that the meetings could be enhanced if a small choir were organized. Soon the choir began regular rehearsals on Wednesday evenings. Mother, Dad, and I were members.

I don't remember if the choir ever actually performed during any Sunday school or worship services. After several rehearsals, however, the members felt that we owed ourselves a party. So the next Wednesday evening a party was held in the home of one of the members. It was so successful that it was decided to have another party in two weeks and invite everyone in town. There was to be a program followed by a dance, and it was to be held in the dance hall over Joe Andreozzi's Silver State Saloon. Joe offered the hall free if we would pay a fee for the lights. (He had his own generator, and the only electric lights in town.)

This party too was a great success, and so another one was scheduled two weeks later, and that established the pattern. Every other Wednesday another party was held. There was always a program followed by a dance. The programs consisted of whatever people were willing to do—there was no lack of volunteers. The town seemed to burst with talent. People dug into their old trunks and produced dozens of humorous monologues, musical numbers, poems, skits, comedy routines, minstrel shows, and one-act plays. Mrs. Wright put on several short musical acts in which I was often paired with June Williams. I really enjoyed those.

The Call family wholeheartedly supported those activities. I remember being in a short play put on by just our family. Dad was the producer and director and also the lead character, a happy cobbler. I played the part of Henry VII of England, Mother was the Queen, . . . and that's about all I can remember about it.

Music for dancing was produced by a volunteer group with a violin, a banjo, a steel guitar, and a "Spanish" guitar, the latter played by Felipe Gonzales. At the end of the evening—usually about midnight since the next day was a workday—a collection was taken up for the musicians who had played for the dancing. Sometime during the evening, there was an intermission and refreshments were served—potluck refreshments furnished by the women in the town.

As more people from the town became interested and showed up for the party, Joe Andreozzi discovered that he had a good thing going. He was selling enough liquor over the bar downstairs to more than pay for the lights, so he offered to provide them for free. And not only the lights: in a burst of community spirit, he began furnishing a large part of the refreshments as well.

Whatever happened to the choir practices? They disappeared, having been replaced by the biweekly community parties.

One might expect that, with Joe's booming liquor business in the saloon downstairs, the dance upstairs would deteriorate into a drunken brawl. That never happened. To us children, Nevada during the 1920s and 1930s seemed to be wide open. Although illegal until the repeal of Prohibition in 1933, liquor was readily available. Joe openly sold drinks over the bar, and the local law enforcement representative, Deputy Sheriff Bill Rutledge, was one of his loyal patrons.

The morals of the time, however, demanded that there be neither drinking nor brawling in the dance hall, and social pressure was generally adequate to enforce this ban. On the rare occasion when someone became offensive, he was promptly ejected and spent the rest of the night in the local jail as a guest of Bill Rutledge. The dance hall was for dancing only. Drinking and fighting were carried on outside.

The practice of hiring babysitters was rare. In Beowawe, entire families would attend the community parties. When the small children grew tired, they were bedded down on and under the benches lining the walls of the dance hall. The older children danced. It was not uncommon to see grown women teaching young boys or men teaching young girls to dance. Dancing was a social occasion. You were expected to mix. Dancing two dances in a row with the same partner was considered boorish behavior.

Our biweekly parties grew bigger and bigger until they included every inhabitant in town and the surrounding countryside—and that was no small feat since Beowawe, in spite of its small size, was a town divided. The town parties, which were held in the dance hall north of the tracks, eventually began attracting the south side boosters. At each event, more and more of the south side would show up. Finally, one Wednesday evening, the last holdout, the proprietor of the south side general store, came to the party.

It was also the last party we held. The next Wednesday Joe Andreozzi's Silver State Saloon and dance hall burned to the ground.

The fire was discovered in the late evening, and although the entire town turned out, it was too late to do anything but watch it burn. It was a spectacular fire. Bottles of Joe's stock erupted in beautiful blue flames, which contrasted nicely with the yellow and orange of burning wood.

After the fire had burned out, Joe cleaned up the mess and built a new place on the same spot. It was a one-story affair with a saloon in front and a small dance hall in the rear. At first he called it the Torre Del Lago Saloon, but he later changed the name. He held dances there, and I went a couple of times, but it was never the same. The community parties were gone forever.

18

Summer Fun — and Work

The first week in May 1933, the school year came to an end, and once again we had the whole summer before us. We swam in the river, of course—several times a day. That year we began swimming in the river in late April, although Rey and I took a fast dip in the river early in March just to make sure we would be the first in town to do so. Actually, we had been swimming all winter, but we had been doing it in the warm pool on the Horseshoe Ranch. The Grayson Hinckley family, who operated the ranch, didn't mind our using their pool when they weren't using it. We hiked out to the Beowawe Geysers six miles or so west of town, a much shorter hike than the one I had taken from Shoshone the first time I saw them. And then there was a two-week period in which I had to go to the emergency airport every day to get Blanco and bring him home.

Oh, yes, Blanco was back with us. I can't remember just when I scraped together enough money to send for him. The young section hand who had taken him had moved from Westwood to Litchfield. He was reluctant to give him up, but was kind enough to send him along anyway. The reason I had to go to the emergency airport for Blanco every day was that he wouldn't stay home. He was in love. It happened that the Williamses, who worked for the government and lived at the airport, had a Spitz bitch, and they thought that Blanco would be the perfect sire for a litter of pups. So when their dog came into heat, they offered to take Blanco for a few days and in turn give us the pick of the litter. When it was time for Blanco to come home, he came willingly enough. But he didn't want to stay.

Every day he would head back to the airport to hang around the Williamses' pet, and every day I would have to go get him. That really wasn't too much of a chore, since I was able to visit with June, who I still thought was the most beautiful girl in the world. Eventually, Blanco quit sneaking off, and I had no excuse to go to the airport. In due time, there was a litter of fuzzy white puppies. I selected an aggressive little male and in gratitude sent it by Railway Express to the man who had kept Blanco for all those months. Sometime during the summer, the Williamses were transferred to Carson City, and I never saw June again.

I missed June and secretly mourned her absence for a while, but then Mrs. Lewis moved into town as the third trick operator and brought her daughter. Though she didn't replace June Williams as the most beautiful girl in the world, Juanita Lewis was certainly a close second, and we became instant friends. And there was an added benefit—Mrs. Lewis hired me to haul the U.S. mail.

Actually, hauling the mail was only a part of the job. As the lowest ranked of the three operators who manned the railroad depot around the clock, the third trick operator, who worked from 12:00 midnight until 8:00 in the morning, was responsible for depot housekeeping.[1] Mrs. Lewis also hired me to do the bulk of that housekeeping. I would go to the station early each morning and sweep up the office and waiting room, empty the ashes from the two space heaters, and carry in wood and coal. I would then flag the early morning passenger train, Number 21, unload incoming mail and express from the train, and load the outgoing mail and express.

Then after the train had gone, I would put the mail into a two-wheeled handcart and take it to the post office. Since the post office was never open at that time of the morning, I left the mail on the front steps and returned the handcart to the station house. No one in town thought it odd that a thirteen-year-old kid was responsible for the U.S. mail from the time it arrived on the train until it was delivered to the post office. And from the time it was delivered until the post office opened, no one was responsible for it. The mailbags just lay there on the steps in plain view.

For this I was paid ten dollars a month. When I got my first month's pay, it was the most money I had ever seen, and I wasted no time in realizing a long-cherished dream. I sent away to Montgomery Ward for a single-shot .22 rifle, and then waited a week of agonizing days for it to arrive. After the second day, I would make an extra trip every day to the Railway Express office (which was nothing more than a shelf in the depot under the grill in the partition dividing the telegraph office from the waiting room). If it had arrived on Number 21, I would have noticed it when I unloaded the express. Mrs. Lewis wouldn't have let me have it, of course, since she wasn't the station agent, but I would have known it was there. Since I didn't know if the package would arrive on a westbound or an eastbound train, I would meet the other local express train, which stopped in the afternoon. For some reason, on the day it finally arrived I hadn't met the train. Dad told me the gun was there when he came home from work. As I proudly carried the unopened box home, I met Ray Arnett, the second trick operator, who was on his way to work.

"Ah ha," he said, "I see you have a new gun."

"How do you know that?" I asked.

"Easy," he replied with a smile. "I've seen a lot of those boxes. Be careful with it. Guns are deadly!"

Dad, who had no love for guns and admitted that he was no expert on gun safety, established three rules:

"Rule number 1: For at least the rest of this year, time to give you experience in handling the gun, you will always go alone when you go out to shoot. That way you will not accidentally shoot someone who is with you. Second rule: Always think before you shoot. You must always know where the bullet will go if you miss your target. Third: Don't ever bring a loaded gun into the house!"

I still have that little rifle. It is old and worn, and it isn't really safe to shoot. I don't believe a round has been fired from it for twenty years.

Leon Sansinena had returned from his year of high school at Eureka, and he and Benito Gonzales resumed a game they had been playing for a couple of years. They began playing the parts of characters taken from *Wild West Weekly Magazine*. This little magazine, printed on pulp paper with a garish cover, cost a dime, and they always bought a copy when it came on sale at Andy Allen's general store. They liked the magazine because there were never any female characters. Females would have interfered with the fast action for which the magazine was noted. The main story in nearly every issue alternated between a character called Kid Wolf and one named Sonny Tabor. In play, as they acted out the roles, Benito was always Kid Wolf and Leon was Sonny Tabor. When I played with them I was always Lum Yates. This character was assigned to me with snickers and mild scorn.

To find out who this Lum Yates was, I bought a copy of the magazine. Dad discouraged us from reading "those junk magazines." "They aren't bad magazines," he told us. "Evil never triumphs in them, and the good characters always come out on top. But there are better things to read."

The issue I had bought carried a Lum Yates story, and I discovered that Lum Yates was neither particularly strong physically nor particularly fast with his six-shooter. Where Kid Wolf would solve his problems with his huge fists, and Sonny Tabor with his lightning draw, Lum Yates overcame his opponents through logic and psychology. I now understood the snickers when I was assigned this role. I also understood why the editors of *Wild West Weekly* never ran a feature story starring Lum Yates. There just wouldn't have been enough blood and guts.

The summer wasn't all fun and games. Early on we found out that Dad's ideas on how we boys were to spend the summer differed from ours, and his ideas weren't all that much fun.

"Starting Monday morning," he told Rey and me, "I want you to dig a new cesspool. The old cesspool is full, and the pit under the outhouse is getting full. I think a single hole can be made to take care of everything."

"Why do you want *us* to do it?" I asked. "The section crew usually does that kind of work."

"Usually they would, but it will be several weeks before the gang can get to it and it ought to be done now. And I don't want you boys to spend the summer in idleness."

Dad took us out into the yard and marked out a spot about six feet square. "When you have the hole six feet deep, you may stop. If you dig two feet a day, you can easily finish it this week. If you get right at it and work steadily, you will still have time each day for other things you want to do."

Monday morning we began. We dug out our two feet and then joined the Gonzales boys and the Sansinena boys down at the river. They had already been swimming once that day—they didn't have to dig a cesspool. The second day, we dug our two feet and went to the Beowawe Geysers. Usually we hiked, but this time Paul Sansinena had gotten an old open touring car to use for the afternoon. When we got home, Dad was standing in the yard looking at our hole.

"It won't do, boys. It just won't do! The hole is crooked. Look at the way the sides bulge out in places, and that far corner isn't even square. You will just have to straighten it up!"

"But, Dad," Rey objected, "when it's covered over, it won't show. It will still do the job!"

"Boys, you're missing the point. Would you like to have everyone in town come over and look at the job you're doing? What about the men from the section crew? Would they dig a hole like this?" We shook our heads, and Dad went on. "I work with men who can't even read or write. But they take pride in the work they do. They take pride in digging a perfectly straight trench or a hole with the sides perpendicular and true. No matter what you do, always do a job you can be proud of. Here, I'll help you straighten it out."

We got into the hole and began to work, but again Dad wasn't satisfied.

"You're not handling your shovels right," he told us. "Don't let the dirt slide off the end of your shovel when you throw it. A man who takes pride in his work drops his shovel out from under the load and the dirt falls in a clump just where he wants it."

We tried it, but discovered that it took extra effort to drop the shovel down from under the clump of dirt. After a while we got the hang of it, and Dad seemed satisfied. In a few days we finished digging that hole the way Dad wanted it, and it was duly covered with railroad ties and topped with a layer of dirt.

I learned a valuable lesson from that experience. In addition to the old adage that "a job worth doing is worth doing well," I learned that proper use of the tools for the job is also important. And I came away from that experience with a lot of respect for any man who could dig a straight trench or a square hole with smooth, vertical sides using only a pick and shovel.

19

A New School

The 1933–34 school year was scheduled to start on September 5, the day after Labor Day. However, on Wednesday evening, August 30, the schoolhouse burned to the ground. There were rumors that the fire might have been deliberately set, perhaps by some of the children who didn't want to go to school, but most likely it was caused by spontaneous combustion. One of the townsmen had been oiling the floors with linseed oil, and he had probably left a pile of oil-soaked rags. It was a spectacular fire, and everyone in town turned out to watch it. Needless to say, most of the children were jubilant. No telling how long it would take them to build a new school!

It didn't take that long. Converting the county garage, located just west of the site of the old schoolhouse, took just a month. The garage was built of railroad ties and was a sound structure. The workmen divided it into two rooms, and a number of windows were cut into the east side to let in light. To allow space for chalkboards, no windows were made on the west side. The inside surfaces of the ties were covered with Celotex, and the outside was covered with wooden siding and painted gray. A bell tower was installed, the boys' and girls' outhouses were relocated from the site of the old school, and, outfitted with new desks, the schoolhouse was ready for use. No time was spent in installing electric wiring or plumbing!

In the meantime, our summer fun continued. We began playing in the old abandoned cinnabar mine a short distance south of town.[1] It was a fascinating place, with tunnels, stopes, and shafts. The tracks and ore car were still in place, and we found that if we pushed the ore car ahead of us we could travel through the black tunnel until we came to a large room that opened to the sky. It was deliciously scary walking along between the rails in complete darkness, pushing that old ore car ahead of us. There were one or two shafts that had been drilled to a lower level, but we knew where they were and were able to avoid them in the dark.

In exploring the structures still standing we happened on the old powder house—at least I think it was the powder house—with some sticks of old dynamite lying about on the ground. Not knowing any better, we picked them up and unwrapped them, but they were so old they had turned to crumbling gray granules. We casually broke them up and scattered the pieces around. Fortunately for us, there was no explosion.

Sometime during the summer, a scout troop was organized in town. Dad was the main booster and had worked hard to get it going. Nearly all of the boys of eligible age joined up.

In September when there was no school, our troop wound up with a community service project. Early in his administration, President Roosevelt had scheduled a "fireside chat" addressed to the Boy Scouts of America. Someone had set up a radio in the town courthouse, where we held our scout meetings, and we all gathered to listen to what the president of the United States and honorary president of the Boy Scouts of America had to say.

In his talk, he urged all scout troops to engage in some sort of special service project, the details of which I no longer remember. Together with our scout leaders, we determined that that particular service was beyond our troop, but some sort of community service was due. So we decided to clean up the Maiden's Grave Cemetery.

The Maiden's Grave Cemetery was a local landmark a few miles southeast of town. During the previous school year, Mrs. Wright (who didn't always get her details straight) had told us how a young girl, Lucinda Duncan, a member of the luckless Donner Party, had died when they had camped near Gravelly Ford, and how her grave was just where the Central Pacific Railroad had wanted to lay its track. She told us how the railroad had compassionately moved her remains up on the bluff overlooking the river and had erected a large cross with her name on it. The people of Beowawe also buried their dead there under the shadow of that cross. For the most part, Mrs. Wright's version was true; however, none of the histories I have read lists Lucinda Duncan as a member of the Donner Party.

So one Saturday we and our scout leaders went up to the cemetery. We cleaned out all the tumbleweeds and other unsightly growth. We repaired the fences around some of the plots, straightened up the sagging headstones and markers, and generally set the whole area in good order. There were enough of us to finish the job on that same day. While it was not exactly the job he had asked for, we felt we had done our best to comply with our president's wishes.

On Monday, October 2, school finally began. Mrs. Carter was now principal and head teacher and taught the upper four grades. There was talk around town that she had convinced the school board that Mrs. Wright was incompetent. I, for one, was sorry Mrs. Wright hadn't come back. She might not have been the greatest of teachers, but she was a cheerful soul, and under her school was often a lot of fun. The lower grades were taught by Miss Theresa Modarelli.

Blithely, we had spent the month of September wringing out the last pleasures to be had from the waning summer. Little did we know that we would be required to make up the time lost. We learned the horrible truth in the early spring, when we were told that school would run through the month of May to make up for the month we had missed at the beginning of the year. Needless to say, few of the children were overjoyed at the prospect. For some time now we had nursed a feeling of superiority over larger schools, whose nine-month schedules kept children in school until the first week of June. Now we were no better off than they were! Our extra month of vacation at the beginning of the year was history and long forgotten. But we soon came up with a scheme to shorten the time.

To Mrs. Carter, we proposed to hold school on Saturdays. As obnoxious as this would be, it would still be better to recover as much of the month of May as possible. Mrs. Carter said she would see what she could do. A few days later she announced that extra school sessions would begin on the following Saturday. Then, on the Friday before Saturday school was to start, we came up with another proposal, which was to cut each class period on Saturday from the usual 40 minutes to 20 minutes; thus we could salvage a half day of free time each Saturday. Strangely enough, the teachers—who obviously loved school and spent as much time there as possible and who always tried to keep children there as well—agreed!

Firm in the knowledge that we had really put one over on the teachers, we thought Saturday school a lark. I don't remember how many Saturday sessions we attended, nor how many May vacation days we recovered. The important thing was that we had won back a measure of our superiority over the larger, duller schools that ground away well into June.[2]

School ended for the year, and I graduated from the eighth grade. The big question for Mother and Dad was what to do about high school. But I wasn't concerned. After all, there was a whole summer to use up before it was necessary to think about school.

Summer is the time for Boy Scouts to go to scout camp. The Nevada Council had a camp not too far from Reno, but for the Beowawe troop that camp was out of the question. There just wasn't enough money available in the town to pay for it. Besides, scouts going to scout camp had to have uniforms, and there wasn't so much as a hat or a neckerchief in town. Dad was certain that a summer camp experience for the boys in town was important, but making it a reality would be a problem.

The solution came in the person of Grayson Hinckley, operator of the Horseshoe Ranch. The Hinckleys were a bit standoffish, but they were generous with their holdings—allowing the town boys, for instance, to use their warm pool, which was fed by hot springs. Grayson Hinckley offered to take the troop up to the North Fork Ranch in northern Elko County for a week's camping. An unemployed telegrapher named Howard Conine was appointed as temporary scout leader. Hinckley also furnished the tents and the transportation, in the form of a one-and-a-half-ton cattle truck.

It was certainly a different kind of scout camp. There was no structured program. We just fished and loafed and did as we pleased. Oh, we took turns helping with the cooking and cleaning and camp maintenance, and twice Howard insisted that we all go down to the creek and take a bath in the cold water.

Fishing was the main order of the day, and everyone except two of us caught fish. Neither Frank Bertrand nor I seemed to have any luck. After the second day without a catch, I got disgusted with fishing and gave it up. I had better luck up on the side hill across the creek hunting rattlesnakes.[3] Frank Bertrand finally caught his one and only fish by jumping into the creek—clothes, shoes, and all—and grabbing a good-size trout with his hands.

Following our week at North Fork, we returned to our summer activities, including swimming in the river. There was no more acting out stories and characters from the *Wild West Weekly Magazine.* This year we were too old for such childish games. Benito and Leon continued to buy the magazine, though.

Blanco was getting old. Yet he didn't think so. He still thought he was young enough to go after a bitch in heat if she happened to be within his range. On occasion this resulted in fights with other dogs, which as usual he always lost. As he aged, he grew stiff in the joints, and on winter mornings especially he would groan when he tried to get up, and it would take him as long as ten or fifteen minutes to get the kinks out. In the late summer of 1934, Dad informed me that it would be cruel to subject poor old Blanco to another one of Nevada's harsh winters. He said it would be kind of us to put him away. Reluctantly, I agreed.

It was not just a simple matter of taking him down to the local animal shelter, saying good-bye to him, and leaving him to his fate. Since there was no such thing as an animal shelter, putting Blanco down was something we would have to do ourselves. Dad asked Joe Andreozzi, who owned a .22 pistol, to shoot the dog while we stood by.

The four of us walked down to a stand of willows by the river, and as we were threading our way through the center of the stand with Joe in front, Blanco moved ahead of me and trotted up to Joe's right side. Joe just reached down, put the muzzle of his pistol close to Blanco's head, and pulled the trigger. We left him where he fell.

A little later, when I was sitting at home trying hard not to cry, Dad suggested that I take a shovel and go back and bury the remains.

"It wouldn't do," he said, "for any of the other children to come across the body, and the dog deserves a decent burial."

I sat there for a few moments, hoping he would offer to come with me. When he didn't, I got up, picked up a shovel, and went back to the stand of willows. When I got to the place where I thought the execution had taken place, I couldn't find him. I carefully searched the entire area. No Blanco, no sign of blood. Nothing.

Maybe the shot hadn't killed him, and he had just gotten up and gone home! I rushed home, fully expecting to see a shaggy, battle-scarred white dog with a bullet hole in the top of his head. But he wasn't there. As I slipped into the house, Rey asked me if I had buried the dog. I just nodded, went past him, and lay down on my bed. I didn't want to talk to anybody.

Some weeks later, when we were alone, Rey said, "You didn't bury Blanco."

"I did too," I retorted hotly.

"No you didn't! I just saw what was left of him in the willows down by the river!"

"It must have been some other dog!" I shouted.

"It was Blanco. I know what Blanco looked like!"

I continued to maintain loudly and heatedly that I had indeed buried the dog. But I knew, and Rey knew, that I hadn't. He dropped the subject and never mentioned it again. Do dogs go to heaven? And—assuming I get there myself—will I meet him someday? And if we do meet, will he look at me sadly and then walk away with drooping tail, or will he do as dogs have always done: forget my failure and come bounding into my wide-open arms?

There have been a few times since then when, due to a serious injury or illness, it became necessary to destroy a family pet. I have always done the job, and then for days afterward I would be an emotional wreck.

20

Montello

In November 1934 Dad moved the family from Beowawe to Montello in Elko County. Montello, ten miles by rail west of the Utah border, had a high school, and his children's continuing education was ensured for at least another few years. I wasn't on hand to help with the move as I was going to school in Utah.

Children graduating from the eighth grade in Beowawe had two choices: they could go away to school or discontinue their education. For some, the eighth grade was as far as they got.

As September approached, Dad and I discussed my future.

"I have arranged for you to go to school in Utah," he told me. "You will live in your grandfather's home in Bountiful. He's not going to charge us board and room, but I have assured him you will do what you can to help pay your way."

"But Dad, I really don't want to go. I think I have had enough school, and besides"—and here I thought I was delivering the clincher—"you only went as far as the eighth grade."

Dad—who spoke English like a college professor, spoke a more literate form of Spanish than most of the Mexicans he worked with, could carry on a conversation in Danish, and even knew a few words of Italian—gave me a long, hard look. Then, looking away to a distant place only he could see, he quietly delivered a clincher of his own.

"I stopped school after the eighth grade because I had no other choice, and I have always regretted it. If I or my father could have arranged it, I would have gone to high school and even to college. My father will take you in and help you through school because he wasn't able to do it for me."

Dad could be very persuasive. The day after Labor Day I started the ninth grade at South Davis Junior High School in Bountiful, Utah. Grandfather still had four children living at home. Beth was two or three years older than I and took the Bamberger school train to Davis High School in Kaysville. Parley and I were both in the ninth grade. Leah and Adelaide were both younger than I. They—my uncle and my aunts—were all embarrassed to have it known that they had a nephew my age, so we agreed that we would be known as cousins. I lived and went to school with my "cousins" for one semester.

I didn't particularly enjoy the school. I had grown used to the closeness of the small Nevada schools, and the impersonal attitude of everyone in the large school depressed me. And then I had to furnish all my own textbooks—a requirement unheard of in Nevada—and I had money enough for only some of them. The few odd jobs I managed to pick up helped, but I was always short of money. Two texts I had to share with Parley, but since we were not always in the same classes that was a problem for me. After all, they were Parley's books.

The problems I was having in school were more than offset by the love I received in Grandfather's home. I was immediately embraced as a member of the family. The homey atmosphere, the things that were done, and the things that were said were all so familiar that I could almost believe I had never left home.

So while I was living in Utah the rest of the Call family moved to Montello. I went home to Montello for the Christmas break. Although it was a strange house in a strange town, it was home, and I decided not to go back to Utah.

Montello was the biggest community we had lived in since coming to Nevada. With a population of about three hundred, it had been established by the railroad to provide helper engines for freight trains to climb the long grade west of town.

In the whole state of Nevada, the SP main line crosses only one hill of any consequence. That hill lies between Wells and Montello, a distance of about fifty-two miles by rail. Trains traveling east from Wells ascend the grade to Moor, a nine-mile climb of 1,000 feet. From Moor to Valley Pass, the trains travel a level stretch of twenty-two miles, then descend to Montello, 1,100 feet lower, a distance of twenty-one miles. The grade from Montello to Valley Pass is only half as steep as that from Wells to Moor. Still, with steam power, helpers were needed to pull the long freight trains up the hill.

To support the helper engines at Montello, an engine house with necessary maintenance shops had been built.[1] This required a rail yard with side tracks and spurs. There was a generator to supply power to the shops and the town, a water tank and water distribution system, a depot and freight house, a company hotel and café for transient train crews, and two track maintenance sections. And of course there were the engineers, firemen, hostlers, roundhouse foremen, boilermakers, car knockers, machinists, yardmasters, signalmen, switchmen, pipe fitters, telegraphers, yard clerks, linemen, section foremen, and gandydancers to keep the whole thing running smoothly twenty-four hours a day.[2] These workers and their families accounted for most of the population.

The town had two general stores, a service station, a pool hall, a barber shop, a café, a dance hall, a concrete jail, and a one-room church. At opposite ends of the town and a short distance away from it were two saloons. They were situated off the section of land occupied by the town since the railroad did not permit the sale of liquor on railroad property. Law enforcement was handled by Justice of the Peace Main Johnson, who also registered voters and operated one of the stores, and Deputy Sheriff Bill Hargrave, who operated the service station. The other store was owned by the Utah Construction Company, which owned and operated the nearby Gamble Ranch and most of the other ranches in the area.

We lived next door to Dr. Arias Belnap, railroad physician, scoutmaster, presiding elder in the local branch of the Mormon Church, and the town's most prominent citizen. You might expect that living in the same neighborhood as the town's foremost citizen would confer special status on the Call family; but that was not necessarily the case. Both houses, ours and the doctor's, were owned by the railroad, and we were assigned the house because it happened to be vacant. The houses were similar in design, except that the railroad had built an extension on the doctor's house for his professional office and a bathroom. Our house had no bathroom and had only cold water until Dad installed a hot water tank, which he connected to the kitchen range.

Every town, no matter its size, seems to develop an upper crust—a group of people who believe they are better, more intelligent, and more refined than the rest of the citizens. Montello was no exception, and the rest of the town, who did not belong, acknowledged the group's superior status with envy, disparagement, or scorn, depending on who was expressing an opinion. Included in Montello's elite were the Arias Belnaps, the Earl Jordans, the Frank Becksteads, the Milo Craigs, the George Culvers, the M. Z. Browns, and the William Hargraves, among others. Mother and Dad were invited to join the group, an honor not ordinarily offered to a mere gandydancer. They considered it briefly.

"We can't accept invitations without doing our share of the entertaining," Dad commented wryly.

"And what would happen," Mother wondered, "if we had a party here and the ladies wanted to 'freshen up?' We couldn't just send them out back!"

Although they liked the people and would have enjoyed the association, they regretfully declined. The Belnaps, however, remained good friends and neighbors.

Dr. Belnap was a fastidious man—too fastidious for some citizens of the town. For instance, he refused to patronize the only barber in town, L. S. Hamm, whose shop was in a front corner room of Lew Killian's pool hall.

"He's old, he's shaky, and he's drunk most of the time," the doctor told Dad. "The one time I let him cut my hair I thought I would pass out from his breath." So Dr. Belnap would get his hair cut on the train. He had a pass that permitted him to ride any car on any train at any time. Every two weeks or so, he would board the noon train, Number 27, have his hair cut by the barber in the club car, get off at Wells, and return to Montello on the afternoon train. It was a unique and satisfactory arrangement; no one else in town could do it. The Call family didn't patronize Mr. Hamm either—Dad cut our hair. I don't remember what Dad did for his haircuts. Maybe he went to Ogden.

Dr. Belnap's evaluation of the town was, "It's a great town for kids—up to the age of eight. After that they ought to be growing up someplace else!" In an effort to improve the lot of boys over the age of eight who weren't growing up someplace else, he organized a scout troop. He was the scoutmaster because there wasn't anybody else to do the job.

One of his first moves was to put every member of his troop into a complete uniform. "Uniforms are important," he believed. "When a kid has a uniform, he knows he belongs."

Very few of the boys in town could afford a uniform. He solved that problem by buttonholing those members of the community who could afford a donation, and by holding a series of entertainments put on by the troop. Soon we all had uniforms, and we looked like a scout troop. And suddenly we began acting like a scout troop.

Dr. Belnap administered nearly all the tests required for advancement, and we soon discovered that there would be no easy road to Eagle rank. As a rule, he accepted nothing less than 100 percent. "When I'm convinced you have done your very best," he told us, "I'll pass you on your tests."

A special trainload of scouts went through one summer day on their way back east to a national scout jamboree. On the train was a much-publicized troop consisting of all Eagle Scouts. That day, Dr. Belnap had gone to Wells for his biweekly haircut, and he decided to ride the special train back to Montello and interview members of this famous troop en route. He came away somewhat disillusioned.

"Any one of my second-class scouts knows more about scouting than that whole troop," he said. And second class was what nearly all of us were. To gain first class rank seemed to take more effort that we were willing to give. We didn't have an Eagle Scout in our whole troop. I believe one boy, Billy King, made it to either Star or Life Scout. If Dr. Belnap was disappointed, he never showed it. Well, almost never—he did mention to Dad once that I should have been senior patrol leader, but he was waiting for me to reach first class. Dad told me about it years later. Dr. Belnap didn't urge or push. He liked self-starters.

As with scouting, he was president of the Montello Branch of the Church of Jesus Christ of Latter-Day Saints because there was no one else.

"I was enjoying Sunday afternoon out at the Pilot Ranch when the brethren came to reorganize the branch," I overheard him tell Dad. "I was relaxing with a cool drink and a cigar when they drove up. When they told me what they wanted me to do, I showed them the drink and the cigar and told them I wasn't interested. After a while they convinced me that I was the one who had to do it. I surely hated to give up those cigars!" As with everything else he did, he took the appointment seriously.

The little one-room church in Montello was used by all denominations. The Protestants had first choice and picked 10:00 A.M. and 7:00 P.M. on

Sundays and 7:00 P.M. on Wednesdays. The Mormons held Sunday school at 9:00 A.M. The Catholics would have a service whenever a priest came to town, which was not often. I was the janitor of the building and tried to have it ready for all meetings. I swept and dusted on Saturday, and in cold weather I built a fire in the potbellied stove early enough to have the room warmed up before a scheduled meeting. There was no water piped to the building, so we didn't have to worry about anything freezing. The railroad furnished coal for heating, and I brought kindling from our woodpile.

Sunday school at 9:00 A.M. and Relief Society on Wednesday afternoons were the only meetings the LDS community held.

"I tried for nearly a year to have sacrament meetings on Sunday," I heard Dr. Belnap tell Dad. "I tried holding it in the afternoon, and I tried it in the evening both before and after the Protestant worship service. Nothing worked; nobody showed up. The attitude of most of the Mormons in this town is, 'Don't bother me. I moved here to get away from the Church!'"

The Belnaps had two children, Bruce and Marjorie. In 1936 Marjorie got sick. In spite of all her father could do, she just got worse. Finally, he put her on a train and took her to the hospital in Ogden, where she died. A short time later, the Belnaps moved to Sparks. It was a great loss to the town.

21

Lee Martin

During the 1934 Christmas holiday, Dad and I walked over to the high school to see about a transfer for me from the Utah school system to Montello. We found Lee Martin, the principal, playing the piano in his office. The door was open, and he motioned us to come in.

"Gershwin's 'Rhapsody in Blue,'" he smiled, and waved at the music sheets on the piano. "It's a tough one, but I'm close to getting it right. Just a little more work. . . . You're Mr. Call, and this is your son, who has been going to school in Utah." He smiled again, shook our hands, and waved us to chairs. He had a good smile, a friendly smile, and I noticed that he had a space between his upper two front teeth that made it all the friendlier. When we told him what we had in mind, he shook his head.

"Now is not a good time for you to change schools," he told me. "You must understand, this is a small school. We have a very limited curriculum. We offer only four subjects for freshmen, and they are required to take all four to fulfill the requirements for graduation. You wouldn't have any problem transferring in English and algebra, and you could probably make up the half year of general science that you are not now taking, but the last subject, Spanish, is a problem. It's a difficult subject, you have missed half a year, and we have no other place to put you. I teach the class myself, and I know what you are up against. I just don't see any way around it."

Dad, looking a bit amused, inquired, "Do you have a Spanish book handy?"

Mr. Martin gave him a slim book with a red cover. Dad handed it to me and said, "Read it aloud."

I then read several paragraphs aloud. I read beautifully. My pronunciation was close to perfect. The only catch was, I had no idea what I was reading. Except for a few words—including some I had learned from Benito Gonzales and was careful never to use where Dad could hear me—I didn't speak or understand Spanish, even though I had been around it all my life.

"Why don't we try this?" Mr. Martin said after I'd finished. "You will attend the regular Spanish class with the other freshmen. You won't get much out of it for a while, but stay in there and try. I'll then meet with you for an hour after school every day, and we will start the course from the beginning. You'll have to work at it at home, and it will be a struggle, but you might possibly make it. I think it's worth a try."

Since I wanted very much to learn Spanish, I agreed that it was certainly worth a try.

In January I started school as a freshman at Montello High School. I tackled Spanish with everything I had, and—although it was tough, the assignments I got from Mr. Martin were long, and I sometimes had to get help in interpretation and translation from Dad—I learned Spanish. It took me just six weeks to catch up to the other freshmen, and another six weeks to work my way to the head of the class. That was my introduction to Leland S. Martin, a man who lived only to teach.

The Montello Consolidated Schools consisted of the high school and grade school, operating in the same building. Lee Martin was principal of both.

The year I started, the high school faculty consisted of three teachers. Mr. Martin taught Spanish and commercial subjects such as typing and bookkeeping; Coach Willard "Speed" Weaver taught history, math, and science; and Miss Audrey Merle Hart taught music and English.[1] The size of the student body varied from year to year between thirty and fifty.[2]

Orchestra was an elective and was good for one-half credit. Orchestra rehearsal was held Mondays, Wednesdays, and Fridays an hour before classes started. Athletics was required and was good for one-fourth credit. Athletics was held after regular classes, Mondays and Wednesdays for the boys and Tuesdays and Thursdays for the girls. As only solid subjects were taught during regular class time, they were worth one credit each toward graduation (for which seventeen credits were needed).

It didn't take long for me to discover that Lee Martin was an autocrat who wielded absolute power within the school system. Where was the friendly smile? It was there, but it lurked behind a completely businesslike façade, peeking out only occasionally.

One day I arrived at school early. As it was a Tuesday, there was no orchestra rehearsal scheduled, but there were strange, fascinating noises coming from the music room. I could hear rhythmic noises, some shuffling and banging, and Mr. Martin counting and then singing the words to a popular song, "Oh, you nasty man, taking your love with an easy hand!" A few days later I found out what was going on in there. Mr. Martin was teaching a group of students to tap dance!

This was a side that I had never expected. Except for that first afternoon in his office, when he was cordiality itself, he had always seemed to be such a stern, businesslike man, ruling the school with strict discipline—and here he was tap dancing. It took me a while to catch on. While he was strictly business during school hours, at other times he was delightful to be with, relaxed and fun-loving—and highly talented.

There was a school board, with a sour-faced man named Ed Gundlach as its head. The only other member I remember was Frank Beckstead. The school board supervised a totally independent school district, but we students all had the impression that the school board set policies in accordance with what Lee Martin wanted. Or perhaps more to the point, the board had no policies and allowed Mr. Martin to run the school to suit himself.

For instance, upon assuming the position of principal, he had changed the high school from an "open campus" to a "closed campus." Under the previous principal, students not actually in class could do as they pleased: leave the school, wander about, or hang around Lew Killian's pool hall, the beanery, or the railroad station. Mr. Martin put an end to all that.

"We have seven periods a day," he told the student body. "None of you has more than four classes. That leaves three periods for study. When not in class you will be at your desk in the homeroom studying. That should provide enough study time here at school so there is no need for homework. Occasional homework may be necessary, but if any of you are consistently taking work home, there's something wrong, and I want to know what it is!"[3]

Leland Stanford Martin was born February 8, 1907, at Copper Mountain, Utah, nine miles east and within sight of Montello. He was the second of two children born to George W. and Mary J. Cameron (or Carmen) Martin.[4] He spent his early years in the little town of Tecoma, Nevada, just two miles west of the Utah border. When the railroad abandoned Tecoma in the early 1920s, the family moved to Wells, leaving behind them the grave of Lee's older brother, Harold, who had died in 1922.

Lee attended high school in Wells and completed his education at the University of Nevada in Reno. His first teaching assignment was at Jarbidge, where he remained one year, and then he taught in the high school at Montello for a year or two before he was appointed principal.

He was a forceful, dynamic man—short (about five feet, four inches tall) and slightly built, but athletic. He turned twenty-eight the year I started school there. He was a bachelor whose only interest, as far as we could discover, was the school. He had been engaged to a girl in the Los Angeles area, and they were about to be married. But sometime during 1934, she was killed in an automobile accident, and he apparently formed no lasting attachments afterward. Not that he didn't like women. He dated frequently, and I remember once when he returned from one of his usual summers spent with his friends in the movie industry in Hollywood, he told us he had met screen seductress Hedy Lamarr at a party. He raved about her.

"She's absolutely beautiful! You see her on the screen, but you just can't imagine what she's like in person!"

My brother Rey had joined the orchestra at the beginning of the school year and had elected to play one of the trombones owned by the school. He spent perhaps a semester in the beginners' orchestra, and then by early 1935 he was good enough to be promoted to the school orchestra, made up of students from both the high school and the grade school.

The state music festival was held in Elko that spring, and although I didn't play an instrument, I decided to tag along. That was no problem. I had a railroad pass, and I found a place to stay with a German family named Binder who had lived in Beowawe. Dad and I attended the orchestra program, held in the Elko High School auditorium. Dad was able to attend because he was relief foreman at Osino, nine miles east of Elko.

I was disappointed by the program. The only music I knew anything about was George Gale's country and western records and the simple songs we had learned in grade school. This music confused me. There were just too many instruments playing all at once, and most of the time I couldn't hear any sort of tune.

"This is awful," I whispered to Dad. "All they're doing is making noise—and they're all pretending it's music!"

"It *is* music!" Dad retorted. "It's good music. Sit still and listen."

I sat and listened, and after a while I began to understand it. Some of it I enjoyed, when I could identify a melody, but mostly it was boring. I was glad when the program was over.

At the end of August, just before school was to begin, Dad told me that the school had bought some new instruments, including a French horn and a cello, and that I ought to try for one. He suggested I put in for the French horn. I didn't have the faintest idea what a French horn was, but I dutifully put my name on the list—and got the horn! Darrel Bullough, a freshman, was the only other student to ask for it, but he settled for a saxophone. I still had no idea what a French horn was until I went to see Miss Hart, who showed it to me. What a fascinating, strange-looking instrument! It had a small, sharp mouthpiece at one end of a long, shiny brass tube that grew bigger as it looped and twisted in a circular pattern to end in a big flared bell.

The mouthpiece, when I put the horn to my lips, felt far different from the bugle I had played in the scout troop in Beowawe. It was tiny and felt almost sharp enough to cut my lip. I tried to blow the horn and got only a croaking, strangled sound—something like the squawk of an angry crow.

"Take it easy," Miss Hart cautioned. "Don't blow so hard! Loosen up. Keep your fingers off the keys, and play a lower note . . . lower . . . lower. Here"—she hit a key on the piano—"play this note."

When I finally played an approximation of the note, she said, "Good. That's an F, the basal tone of the instrument. All of your music will show it as middle C. Here's a fingering chart and some exercises. Go home and practice, and I'll see you at this same time a week from today."

I put the horn back in its awkward-looking case and carried it home. I don't know how Mother and Dad stood it for the next few weeks. Grant was playing one of the school's violins; Rey was playing the trombone. With me starting on the horn, and all of us trying to practice at the same time, it must have been difficult for them. True, each of us was in a different room, but the house was small, the conflicting sounds carried, and there was no getting away from them. Yet they endured, and all we heard from them was encouragement. Dad finally worked out a schedule so that only one of us was practicing at a time. While one practiced, the others were doing necessary chores, and as we got better the results were easier to bear.

For a few weeks I played in the beginners' orchestra; then Miss Hart moved me up to the main orchestra. I was really making great progress, I thought, until Mr. Martin stopped in at a rehearsal and listened for a few minutes.

After she cut us off, Miss Hart turned to him. "Well?" she asked.

"It's coming along very well, except the French horn is out of tune."

"I know," she said. "I was anxious to have that horn here, and I moved him up before he was quite ready. He's learning fast and does very well—when he pays attention." She was looking right at me when she said that last part, and I could feel the heat rising up out of my shirt collar. I had been paying more attention to June Beckstead, our only cellist, than to the music. Miss Hart had placed us side-by-side in the center of the group, and I found her to be, well, distracting. She was pretty, but awfully young. She was still in grade school.

So why was I paying attention to her instead of one of the high school girls? One reason was that girls my age frightened me, and another reason was that the high school girls all seemed to be too involved to pay any attention to me. At Montello, as at nearly every other school I went to in Nevada, the boys outnumbered the girls.[5]

A whole new world began to open up for me. As the orchestra played music by Handel, Debussy, Brahms, and Mozart, and I struggled to match what I was playing to the tune carried by the rest of the instruments, I began to understand and appreciate great music. Our little orchestra was far from expert, and some of the passages we played with such fervor were more dissonant than harmonious, but to me it was all great stuff. The awful noises I had endured at the music festival the previous spring were now the most beautiful sounds I had ever heard!

Lee Martin spent his summers in Los Angeles and Hollywood, mingling with friends in the film industry. He would come back from those visits full of ideas for drama and dance presentations. Each of the several dance routines he taught during the year had to have its own stage setting. One set for an entire program just wouldn't do. They didn't do it that way in Hollywood, and he wasn't about to do it in Montello. If there were five dances, there were five separate sets, each having to be designed, built, and then set up on the stage for each number.

He discovered that I had some ability for design and drafted me to help him. It started when he needed a picture to go on the rear wall of a stage set he was putting together for a three-act play he was directing.

"I have hunted all over town," he told me, "and I can't find anything with the right color combinations." He handed me a desk-size calendar with a small reproduction of a lighthouse. "These colors are just right. Do you think you can copy it? It needs to be about eighteen by thirty inches."

I was dubious. "I'll sketch it in pencil, but I won't color it. I don't use colors." I hadn't tried to paint or color anything since my fourth grade teacher, Parmel, had slapped me in the face. Not even when Mrs. Wright, my seventh grade teacher, had threatened to downgrade a pencil sketch of two hunting dogs I had done unless I colored it.

"If you will lay it out, I'll get Miss McQuiston to fill in the color," he told me. I completed the sketch and took it to Miss McQuiston, who taught the seventh and eighth grades.

"That's really good," she said. "But it would be a shame if you didn't go ahead and finish it yourself."

"I can't paint. Nothing ever comes out right. When I try to add color to a sketch, especially with watercolors, it looks awful, and I just throw it away."

She opened a desk drawer and took out a small, flat box. "I know just what you mean about watercolors," she said. "They can be difficult. But maybe you could try something else, like these pastels."

She then showed me how the pastels could be blended, and how one color could be applied over another without running, and how easily a mistake could be corrected.

"Try it," she urged, "and if you really can't do it, bring it back and I will finish it."

What she had shown me looked fascinating, and with some trepidation, I took the sketch and her box of pastels and started to work—and, wonder of wonders, the picture actually started to take shape! The colors began to live! They went just where I wanted them, and they blended just right! I finished the picture and was amazed. Did I really do that? I took the picture back to Miss McQuiston, who looked at it critically, praised it—and then gave me the box of pastels to keep. Now there was a great teacher!

A native of Nevada, Marguerite McQuiston was one of those dedicated teachers often found in the tiny Nevada schools in those years. She was the teacher who had finally convinced my brother Grant that he could do better in school and encouraged him to try. She had now helped two members of my family—and I wasn't even one of her students! I still have that box of pastels.

I began to help Lee Martin design and build his dance sets. I also designed and supervised the decorations for the annual Junior Prom for the years 1937, 1938, and 1939. The Junior Proms in those days were not just for students and faculty. Anyone who had the admission price was invited, and people came from as far away as a hundred miles just to see what new and startling decorating ideas we had come up with. Each year's decorations were more elaborate and more expensive than the previous year's. Admissions were expected to pay for the decorating.[6]

After all the work I put into them, I didn't enjoy those Junior Proms. June Beckstead had moved with her family to Imlay, and I was too shy to ask anyone else for a date. I would go to a dance, watch and listen for a while, and then go home. The dance was a success. My part of it was finished.

22

Crickets

"How would you like a job for the summer that pays five dollars a day?" Dad asked me one day toward the end of June 1936. He was looking rather pleased with himself, and with good reason. Five dollars a day was two dollars more than he made when he worked as a gandydancer.

"I'd like that," I replied, "but who is going to pay me that kind of money? And what would I have to do for it?"

"You would be killing Mormon crickets, and your pay would come from the WPA.[1] You will have to leave home, though, and live in a camp all summer, and you will work seven days a week including holidays."

I had planned to spend the summer working on that French horn. I had talked the school into letting me keep it for the summer, and I had been rehearsing with the Ray Minter Band in Ogden every Saturday.

A job with the Cricket Control Project would cancel those plans, but there was really not much choice. The job was available because Dad had a large family and little income, and the extra money was sorely needed. So early the following Monday, June 29, Earl Faro, who was also going to work on the project, gave me a ride to Elko. Regretfully, I left the horn at home.

Upon arriving in Elko, we had an interview with the project director, Bud Lukey. We bought personal items, such as high boots and toilet articles, and got the first of two required "tick shots"—inoculations for Rocky Mountain spotted fever, spread by wood ticks. On Tuesday, Earl and I threw our bedrolls into the back of a stake bed truck, climbed in, and made ourselves comfortable on top of a load of supplies. As the project discouraged private transportation, Earl left his car in Elko. Delbert L. Pruitt, the foreman and our new boss, rode in the cab with Jim Ford, who owned the truck and drove it under an arrangement with the project.

As the new road up East Adobe Creek was not yet open, we took the old unpaved road out of Elko, winding up the face of the Adobe Range. I remember passing Dinner Station and crossing the Independence Mountain range. We passed the Tuscarora turnoff and went through Jack Creek and Deep Creek, finally arriving at the cricket camp on Bull Run Creek five miles south of White Rock. The eighty-mile trip had taken about four hours.

The camp was located a half mile east of the road under some trees a few hundred yards south of the creek. It consisted of two tents: a cook tent and a bunk tent. Since the bunk tent was full, I had to unroll my bed on the ground under the trees. I slept in the open for a few days until Del Pruitt was able to borrow another tent from the SL Ranch.

The gang consisted of about twenty men. At sixteen, I was the youngest. Del Pruitt was from Montello, as were about a third of the crew, among them Everett Whipple, Jack Craig, Don MacCleod, Earl Faro, Jack Canfield, Sinibaldo Benedetti, and Hank Smith, the camp cook.

Hank Smith wasn't the greatest of cooks, and he hated to make any kind of dessert. Finally, after considerable complaining from the gang, he attempted a few cherry pies. I watched him as he poured the cherries out of a gallon can directly into the pie shells. I don't know how he made the pie crusts. The consensus of the camp was that they would have made good roofing shingles or paving tiles. They were a bit too stiff for tire patches.

There were crickets all over, wandering around the camp and poking their chitinous noses into everything. And they would make a crackling noise when I accidentally stepped on them. At first I would jump each time it happened, and I began watching where I stepped. I soon realized that I couldn't keep that up for the rest of the summer and tried to ignore them.

"What about all these crickets? Can't we get rid of them?" I plaintively asked as they began to get on my nerves.

"Ah, they're just strays." Everett Whipple answered. "They aren't thick enough to bother with. Tomorrow we'll show you some real swarms!"[2] At 3:00 the next morning my first day of killing Mormon crickets began.

The Mormon cricket, of the order Orthoptera, is native to parts of Utah and Nevada. The insect is always in the area, but usually it is not noticeable and causes little damage. Occasionally, when conditions are just right, the crickets will begin to multiply wildly and migrate in dense bands, devastating all green and growing things in their search for food. Although they prefer tender forage such as alfalfa, they will eat anything they can chew apart. More than once I have waked from a sound sleep because one of the wretched things was chewing on my ear. Nor do they hesitate to eat each other.

"These things are cannibals," one of the men told me the first day on the job. "Look here." With a sharpened stick he cut off the abdomen of one of the crickets as it was going past. The wounded cricket just kept on walking, but immediately two of its fellows moved behind it and began snacking on the open wound. All three of them continued to walk along.

"Rotten bastards. It's enough to make you puke!" he growled as he crushed the insects under his boot.

Bands of crickets were first spotted in parts of Elko, Eureka, and Lander Counties in 1935. I had heard stories of how massive bands had caused railroad locomotives to lose traction and cars to slide off highways. Sporadic efforts were made to eliminate them, but these were largely ineffective. It was not until 1936 that a serious effort under federal and state auspices was started.[3]

Hatching in April, the crickets are green and about a quarter inch in length. As they grow, they shed their skins, and with each skin change they change color. When I arrived at the end of June they were one to one and a half inches in length and were a light reddish brown. At the end of July, when they reach maturity and begin to mate, they are dark brown or black. The male at maturity is the length of a large grasshopper, but several times as heavy. The mature female is the same size or a bit larger, except she has a long tail, an ovipositor, resembling a curved yellow saber, which doubles her overall length.

By 4:30 that first morning, we were all set to start killing crickets. We had already eaten breakfast. We had loaded all our gear into Jim Ford's truck and had traveled a few miles to a spot where a band of crickets had been spotted. We had unloaded our dust spreaders and barrels of poisonous dust from the truck and had filled the reservoirs of the dusters. We were now waiting for enough light to see.

As the early morning brightened, we could see movement as the insects began their march in constant search of food. We strapped on our dusters, put on our dust masks, and began moving across the band perpendicular to their direction of travel. The dusters were horizontal cylinders, perhaps a foot in diameter and a foot long. On the right was a crank that operated a blower, and on the left was a tube with a nozzle that could be swiveled close to the ground. We walked across the front of the band in a straight line, about four to six feet apart, turning the cranks and blowing the dust in clouds on the moving insects. When we reached the other side of the band, we pivoted on the last man in line, spread out, and crossed the band again.

The dust was sodium arsenic mixed with quicklime. Besides the dust masks, we also wore long-sleeved shirts with collars buttoned, and pants tucked into high boots or tied tightly around the boots at the ankles. The dust mixture didn't kill instantly. The theory, as explained to me, was that the quicklime caused discomfort to the insects, who then tried to lick it off, thus ingesting a sufficient amount of arsenic to kill them within two or three days.

As the morning wore on, the work began to cause me discomfort. The straps of the duster dug into my shoulders, my right arm ached from turning the crank, and my nose inside the dust mask itched. Finally Everett Whipple, who was in charge of our group, called for a brief break. As the morning grew warmer, those welcome breaks became more frequent—not that he felt we needed the rest, but we had to keep from sweating due to the clouds of quicklime dust, which caused burns on damp skin.

Finally at about 10:00 we ran out of crickets, and he called a halt. We loaded up our equipment and went back to camp. Our noon meal was served at 11:00, after which we took our leisure about the camp until 3:30 in the afternoon, at which time our evening meal was served. We then went out and worked another three hours until it got too dark to see. That was the pattern for the next few days. We avoided the heat of the day because of the dust hazard.

We weren't always dusting. If a band was thick enough, we would build a cricket fence in front of it. The fence consisted of galvanized steel sheets a foot wide and ten feet long. A series of surveyor's stakes were driven into the ground, two stakes together, so that they stood no higher than nine inches. The steel panels were then inserted between the stakes. The panels overlapped at the ends between each set of stakes. Depending on the width of the approaching horde, the fence could be any length from a quarter mile to a mile and a half. If the ground was not too rocky, pits were dug at intervals. The openings to the pits were covered with overhanging lengths of steel sheets bent so that the crickets could slide into the pit but couldn't crawl out. In stony ground, traps were formed from the steel sheets. They were perhaps six to ten feet across with ramps built next to the fence to entice the crickets up to a slide, where they then slid into the traps. At the sides of the ramps opposite the fence, wings were built to guide the crickets to the ramps.

"Just like catching wild horses," said one of the men, who had spent several years catching wild mustangs for a living.

The fences were very effective. The Mormon cricket cannot fly, and it can jump only a few inches. The crickets could climb up the wooden stakes, but as long as the tops of the stakes were three inches below the top of the fence, they couldn't climb over. When they came to the fence, they would move along it until they fell into a pit or a trap. What happened, I wondered, when the pits and traps got full? I soon found out.

"Tomorrow it will be your turn to help Jack Craig maintain the cricket fences," Del told me one day during the evening meal. "If you like it, you can have the job permanently." No one said anything, but I got some strange looks from the other men.

The next morning, the truck dropped Jack and me off near one of the fences. As we approached the fence, the wind was blowing toward us, and cool as it was in the early morning, the stench was horrible. I gagged and very nearly lost my breakfast. We were carrying shovels, a kerosene weed burner, and a five-gallon can of kerosene. Jack directed me to take a shovel, go along the fence, and repair any spot where the crickets could crawl under the fence. As I did this, he started up the weed burner and began burning the crickets inside the traps. As the morning warmed up, the smell from those traps got worse.

The traps seemed to be half to three quarters full of a writhing mess consisting of a layer or two of live crickets that appeared to be crawling or swimming on top of a thick soup of dead crickets, cricket juice, and maggots. In the center of each trap was a mound of gray ash. Jack used the weed burner to reduce the crickets to ashes, and then with shovels we piled the ashes up in the centers of the traps. It was nauseating work, and I soon lost my breakfast. Jack, it turned out, was the only man on the crew who could work around those traps without getting sick, and even he had problems.

"Time or two, I had to go up on the side hill and sit for a while to let my stomach settle down," he told me. "Where we have pits, it's easier. We just cover them over and dig new ones."

When it came time to go in for dinner, I wasn't a bit hungry. "Better eat something anyway," Jack said. "You'll need it."

Unlike the dusting crews, Jack and I went back to the fences right after our meal and worked during the afternoon. Even though it was hotter, and the smell was worse, I didn't lose my dinner. I spent considerable time up on the "side hill," though.

"Well, do you want the job?" Del asked me that evening. I respectfully declined.

I remember one fence in the White Rock area that was a mile and a half long. Crickets, like a dark blanket covering everything, glided down the mountain against that fence for three weeks. When they finally stopped coming, the twenty-three traps along that fence had mounds of ashes nearly three feet high. In his report, Del Pruitt estimated that more than ten thousand bushels of crickets were captured by that one fence.

We also used fences to shield ranch houses and outbuildings. We had just finished our noon meal one day, and were getting ready to relax for the afternoon, when one of Jake Reed's boys drove up to our camp.

"We're being invaded!" he shouted. "We're trying to hold them back with noise, but they're gaining!"

While some of the crew went in Jim Ford's truck to get fencing materials, the rest of us piled into the Reed pickup and headed for their ranch on Winters Creek. What we saw when we got there was amazing. A bare hill a short distance behind the ranch house, normally a gray-yellow color, had turned black. The ground between the hill and the ranch house was also black with crawling insects.

Everyone at the ranch was moving across the front of the band, beating on pots, pans, five-gallon oil cans, and anything else that would make a noise, but there weren't enough of them, and they were losing ground. We grabbed whatever noisemakers we could find and joined the parade. Strangely enough, the noise frightened the insects and turned them back, but only for a few seconds. It was necessary to keep it up continually to hold them at bay. A few minutes later, the truck arrived with the rest of the crew and the fencing, and we quickly built a fence to shield the ranch buildings.

Two weeks after I arrived, Bud Lukey drove out from Elko with our paychecks. Fifteen days' pay amounted to seventy-five dollars, and there were no deductions. It was the most money I had ever seen. But bringing our pay wasn't the only thing Bud had on his mind.

"Where's Benedetti?" he asked. "I'm ready for that fishing contest." Sinibaldo Benedetti, a cousin of Adolfo Benedetti, who was Dad's boss in Montello when Dad wasn't relieving another foreman, had been taking an afternoon once or twice a week to fish in Bull Run Creek, supplying trout for supper. Bud, who considered himself to be an expert fisherman, was present at one of those suppers and proposed a fishing contest the next time he came to camp.

Benedetti, a short, skinny, middle-aged bachelor with a pinched face, showed up with his fishing gear, and they agreed that the one with the most fish at the end of an hour's fishing would be the winner. They went down to the creek, and in an hour Bud came back with twelve beautiful trout.

"Is Benedetti back yet? We were fishing together, but then he gave me the choice of going up- or downstream and he would take the other way. I decided to go downstream. We separated, and I haven't seen him since. Look at these beauties! He'll have a hard time beating this catch."

"Well, he's right there behind you," one of the men said. And there was Benedetti, lugging a burlap bag into camp. When he dumped it out, his total came to sixty-three fish. For supper we had almost more fish than we could eat.

"I thought I was a fisherman," Bud said, ruefully shaking his head, "but that little shrimp is something else. I don't see how he does it! What's he got down there, a fish farm?"

We didn't stay long on Bull Run Creek. Del Pruitt found a more suitable campsite on a creek north of the White Rock store. The trees were bigger and the shade more plentiful, and it was much closer to water. I have forgotten just where it was. It was probably on Mitchell Creek, but it may have been Wall Creek or Indian Creek. We used the creek water for everything: drinking, cooking, washing, and bathing. We took the water just where it tumbled out from under a heavy overgrowth of brush, and we thought that was the sweetest, best-tasting water in the state—until a week or two later, when someone thought of exploring above that stand of brush and found a dead sheep in the creek.

At the end of July or the first week of August, the crickets were maturing and were beginning to mate. One of the old-timers who had worked the year before described the mating process.

"Ever' morning when the herd starts out," he told us newcomers, "the males are working in the lead and moving fast as they can. They know the females are right behind them, and they want no part of what comes next. When a female catches a male, they curl up together with their hind ends touching, and they work back and forth for a while, until the male lets go his seed. He doesn't want to give it up, see—she just takes it away from him.

"It comes out in a kind of waxy bag that hangs onto her hind end just below and on both sides of that long sword tail. It looks just like a couple kernels of hominy a-hanging there.[4] When she's through with him, the male crawls off looking pretty well done in, and a lot skinnier than he was before he got caught.

"Over the next two, three days that sperm package must look mighty good to the female because she eats it. She just curls around a twig or a blade of grass and chews away at it. In maybe a couple weeks there's no more males left—they've all died off, and the females are busy laying eggs. They just stick that sword tail in the ground and lay maybe a hundred eggs in a nest. They keep that up 'til the frost gets them. Each female can make several nests."

My own observations in the next few days confirmed the accuracy of his account. The males were indeed reluctant. Some reports describe the females eating the males during or right after mating, but I have never seen that happen.[5] Darrel T. Gwinne, reporting on a study of Mormon crickets in eastern Utah and western Colorado, doesn't mention it. He states that the male's spermatophore (about one-fifth of his body weight) provides enough nutrients to satisfy the female.[6]

Gwinne also reports a difference in courting habits in bands of differing population densities. In bands with low-density populations the male starts out by singing for a few minutes to attract females, then leaves his perch and approaches a female, who may accept or reject him. In bands with high-density populations the male sings, but when he leaves his perch, he moves away from the females, who follow and court him. He then makes a choice among those females.[7] Now I have never heard a Mormon cricket sing. In the super-high-density populations of northeastern Nevada, the males didn't bother to sing—they just ran.

Before the summer was over, I was sick of crickets. The last week of August, I caught the southbound mail stage to Elko and took the train to Montello. The next week I started my junior year in high school. As the work had been provided to help out the family, I turned all of my summer's wages over to Mother, except for what I needed to buy clothes for school.

In June of the following year I was back on the Cricket Control Project, back at White Rock, and back working for Del Pruitt. The summer of 1937 was a repeat of 1936, except there was no dead sheep in the creek where we took our drinking water—or maybe 1937 was the year we found the dead sheep after all. It was a long time ago, and my memory is a bit hazy.

23

Johanne

In September 1937, when I was a senior, Mother started high school as a freshman. She went to high school for two years, but had to quit after her sophomore year because she was pregnant—but that's getting ahead of the story.

We were seated around the supper table one evening the week before the 1937–38 school year was scheduled to begin when she announced that she was about to realize a secret ambition.

"When school starts next Tuesday, I'm starting the ninth grade. I'll be going to classes just like the rest of you!"

We were speechless. Our mother in school? Just like one of the kids? It was incredible!

"Will they *let* you go to school?" Rey finally choked out.

"Mr. Martin says yes. He asked me if I was a U.S. citizen. When I said I was, he said he couldn't stop me from going to school."

"But what will Dad say?" Dad wasn't with us that evening. He was out of town relieving a foreman somewhere to the west. But Mother was prepared for that one.

"We've already talked about it. All he said was, 'That's wonderful. Do it!'"

"But why do you want to go to school?" Grant asked.

"Because I'm ignorant. I was taken out of school when I was fourteen to help in the laundry. There was so much I wanted to learn, but I had to leave school and go to work.

"Actually," she continued, "I've been going to school since January. I went over to the school, and Miss McQuiston gave me some tests. They showed that I needed to work on some subjects in the sixth, seventh, and eighth grades. So I've been going over there for lessons after school and studying when you've all been in school. Now I'm ready for high school!"

Well, that at least cleared up a mystery. We had seen her on occasion, coming or going, and we had wondered who she was checking up on and why. We were sure someone in the family must be having some real problems for her to be over there so much. At least we could now relax on that score.

On Tuesday morning, September 7, 1937, Mother, a month before her forty-seventh birthday, started regular classes as a freshman. I was embarrassed. For a woman that age to go to high school was unheard of. Both Rey and I were upperclassmen, and it gave me a strange feeling to watch Mother get up from her desk in the homeroom and go to algebra class with her fourteen-year-old classmates. I cringed; but if Mother, who always had our love and respect, and whose decisions we had learned to regard as right, wanted to go to school, that was her privilege. Fortunately for me, I had the good sense to swallow my embarrassment and say nothing about how I felt. She more than made up for it.

Soon we were all hearing how she was invigorating the classes she attended, how she was stimulating both teachers and students to think. She asked penetrating questions, she raised pertinent issues that weren't being adequately covered, and she made at least one of the teachers uncomfortable. Coach Tharp, who taught world history, for instance, found that he had to be thoroughly prepared for every class she attended. With her Old World background, she was an expert on world history.

Even Mr. Martin had what he thought was a problem—she received a perfect score on her first Spanish test.

"I went over your paper at least three times," he told her. "I couldn't find so much as a misplaced accent or a missing tilde. All I can say is that it wasn't a very good test. A good test ought to show what students don't know as well as how much they do." So, from then on, he made sure that his tests had at least one question he was sure she couldn't answer.

For three semesters, she maintained what I believe was the highest grade point average in the history of Montello High School. We were justly proud of her.

Our mother was born October 4, 1891, in a small village near the city of Aalborg, Denmark. She was the daughter of Frederick Karl Jorgensen and Mette Marie Elizabeth Willesen. They named her Johanne (Yo-HAN-uh) Oline Schantz Jorgensen, a rather long name for a tiny girl, but they had high hopes for her. Her great-grandfather, Peder Schantz, was the son of a French nobleman who had fled France during the Revolution to avoid a group of citizens who were anxious to see how his neck would fit the slot of their brand-new guillotine.

Her earliest years were spent in a small house with dirt floors.[1] When Mother was about three, her father, Frederick, got a job delivering milk and cream for a dairy on the outskirts of the city of Aarhus. He made his rounds pushing a handcart and poured the milk from cans into the customers' own containers. To the delight of Mother Mette Marie, the family moved into a house with wooden floors.

The floors were unfinished hardwood planks with a velvety texture acquired through much scrubbing. Each Saturday, Mette Marie would sweep the floor clean; then with sand purchased from the sandman, she would scrub the floors using gallons of water.

When Mother was still small, Frederick got a better job working on the docks, and the family moved into town, to a house with polished floors.

Although the job paid better, unloading coaling ships was harder, more hazardous work. Frederick was given a barrel fitted with straps. Down in the hold of the ship, the barrel was loaded with coal, and by putting his arms through the straps, he carried the barrel on his back up ladders and onto the dock, where the coal was dumped out. One day as he was climbing one of those steep ladders, he fell and bit through his tongue. The wound never healed, and he died some months later from a related cancer, leaving a young widow and six small children.

To aid her in caring for herself and her children, the state helped Mette Marie start a laundry. She was a loving mother, but not a good businesswoman. Her customers soon learned that they could not count on getting their clean laundry back as promised; while they were waiting for clean shirts and sheets, Mette Marie would likely be out in the forest with her children, gathering berries or wildflowers.

As her business evaporated, she found that she could not care for all her children, so some of them were farmed out to relatives. Mother went to live with an aunt and uncle who also operated a laundry. Although Mette Marie lived until Mother was sixteen, Mother never returned to her home except to visit.

Mother, as a poor relative, was expected to spend her time when not in school helping out in her foster family's laundry. When she was fourteen and of legal age, they took her out of school to work in the laundry full-time. One day the delivery girl quit, leaving baskets of undelivered laundry. Mother pointed out that she knew the customers and that she could deliver the laundry. That became her job for the next several years—carrying heavy baskets of laundry, sometimes for several blocks, and then having to climb two or three flights of stairs to make her deliveries. She told us how on occasion a basket would be so heavy that she had to set it down every few steps to rest, and how in winter she would suffer from chilblains because she didn't have gloves. Her foster parents weren't deliberately cruel, she assured us, but as a poor relative she was expected to work to earn her keep.

When she was in her early teens, missionaries from America visited the family, and in strange accents told them the story of the Church of Jesus Christ of Latter-Day Saints. During their visit Johanne was not invited to sit with the rest of the family, but sat by the door. At fifteen years of age, she asked for baptism. Her foster parents also converted, but later, hearing how Mormons were despised by many in the community and fearing that it might affect their business, they quietly left the church. Mother, like so many European converts of that day, decided to emigrate to America and make a new life for herself in Utah.

At nineteen, she left Denmark, and by way of Hull, Liverpool, Quebec, and Niagara Falls, entered the United States. The trip by train to Salt Lake City was exciting, but it took such a long time she thought it would never end. And from Salt Lake City she took still another train south to Centerfield, where she had relatives. A short while later, seeing that she was more of a burden than a help to that struggling rural family, she moved to Ogden and worked as a domestic servant for several of Ogden's prominent families. Then she was able to secure a position with the Utah State School for the Deaf and Blind in Ogden—working in the laundry.

She enjoyed her stay at the School for the Deaf. There were a number of other young people there, and they enjoyed socials and outings together. Among them was a young man who was working as a stationary fireman at the school. He was brash, impudent, and conceited, and she didn't like him.

Nevertheless, on December 13, 1916, they were married in the Salt Lake Temple.

Almost immediately, he was called on a mission for the church, serving in the Spanish American Mission in Colorado and New Mexico. She supported him on his mission by working in a meat packing plant in Ogden during the two and a half years he was gone. When he was released in late summer of 1919, they set about the serious business of raising a family. I was born in May of the following year, and my brothers and sister arrived in succession.

Although the years spent in Nevada were hard, and the climate was so different from that of cool, green Denmark, Mother learned to love the desert, as shown by the last verse of one of her poems:

A desert moon—a starlit sky,
A merciless blazing sun.
The heart of the desert has claimed my love.
With it I may now be one.

The high grades she got in high school did not come easily. "It's so hard for me to learn anything now," she mourned. "Things came so easily when I was young, and I remembered everything. Now I have to struggle to learn what I need for my next lesson. I have to work so hard just to remember it."

And work she did. I remember coming home late in the evening more than once to find her at the kitchen table studying—or sometimes asleep with her head on her textbook. At the slightest noise, she would open her eyes, sit up straight, sigh a little, and send me off to bed. Early in 1939, things became much harder for her. To her great surprise, she discovered that she was about to add another child to the family, more than eleven years after the last one. When she told us, it was a bigger shock than her announcement that she was going to school. Here we were, a self-contained family that had been together—a solid unit, ever since any of us could remember—and now she was about to bring in a stranger. Our mother was just full of surprises.

Lying on my desk as I write this is a copy of the Permanent High School Record for a student named Call, Johanne (Mrs.). For the two semesters of the school year 1937-38 she received A's in English I, algebra I, world history, and Spanish I. (Remember, this was a small school, and these were the only subjects taught to freshmen that year.) For the first semester of the next school year, she was awarded A's in Spanish II, English II, general science, and plane geometry. However, for the second semester she received three B's and retained an A in only one subject, English.

“How do you account for the difference in her grades for that last semester?” I asked my brothers and my sister at a family gathering not long ago, as I showed them Mother’s school record. They had to think a moment, and suddenly their puzzled frowns were replaced by broad grins. “Of course,” they chorused, “she was pregnant!”

In 1939, for a student to stop school because she was pregnant was usually a subject of deep family shame. But in this instance it was a subject of family pride and delight.

24

Lakeside

There were only three in my graduating class of 1938. Even for Montello that was a small class. As it was customary to assign speeches to the four or five students with the highest scholastic averages, we each had to prepare and deliver a speech at the graduation exercises. Norma Sanders delivered the valedictory, and I was the salutatorian. Lawrence Richards gave a speech predicting how each member of the class would turn out (it was a short speech).

After graduation, I went to Elko to try to get back on the Cricket Control Project for the summer. The project had changed, however. The federal government had pulled out of the program and left it entirely to the state. Bud Lukey was no longer in charge, and I was told they didn't need anymore help. I hung around Elko for a few days until my money ran out. Once I followed Senator Pat McCarran as he strolled through the Commercial Hotel casino greeting some of his constituents. I didn't follow him very far. One of the dealers decided I was underage and told me to leave.

Back in Montello, I picked up odd jobs like mowing lawns, cleaning out weeds from backyards, and distributing magazines. I had regular customers in town for the *Collier's* and *Saturday Evening Post* weekly magazines, but I also ordered extras, which I sold to train passengers. As Montello was a scheduled stop of about ten minutes, it was customary for passengers to get off the train and walk up and down the platform.[1] I would meet the afternoon trains on the day the magazines were released, and I usually sold several since the news butchers added five cents to the cover price, doubling it. The magazines were delivered by Railway Express, and I did especially well if I could talk M. Z. Brown, the station agent, into letting me have the magazines a day early.

When school started in September, Norma Sanders and I went back to school. In 1937 the Montello school district had absorbed the surrounding smaller schools and was able to hire more teachers and expand the high school curriculum. The new teachers were Miss Myna Turner, who taught typing and business courses, and Noble Revier Palmer, who taught manual training, mechanical drawing, and advanced math (algebra II and solid geometry).[2] Norma and I entered as postgraduate students at no cost to us. I was able to take a second year of mechanical drawing and also enrolled in the advanced math class. I continued to play the school's French horn since nobody else wanted it.

I resumed designing and building stage sets for Lee Martin, and I also designed the decorations for the Junior Prom; however, this year I got paid for it, as Lee Martin had some National Youth Administration funds to disburse.[3] The design for the Junior Prom decorations that year called for a series of arches with several variations in the ratio of the height to the base. The design included a band shell on the stage, almost a quarter of a sphere, based on three intersecting curves, none of them a true quarter circle. Laying out and building all those arches and curves took so much time that I neglected to complete several of the drawing assignments in my drafting class.

At the end of the course, when I mentioned to Mr. Palmer that I was short several assignments, he said, "Let me see your Junior Prom sketches."

I gave him all my sketches, some of them freehand, done on whatever scrap of paper I had available at the time.

"What you've done here is a practical application of what you've learned in the course. Your arches and the band shell are areas we didn't even cover," he told me, and he solemnly graded each one of them. I passed the course with an A for the first semester and a B for the second.

In June, after school ended for the year, two events affecting the Call family took place almost at the same time. I went to work for the railroad as a gandydancer, and Dad successfully bid on the Strongknob section, located on the mud flats in Utah west of the Great Salt Lake. The rest of the family moved to Lakeside, Utah, and I moved into a room in an old building in the next block west of where we had lived for five years. My new boss was John Tofanelli, foreman of the Tecoma section.[4] The first day on the job was spent tamping ties.

The objective of every section foreman was to have a perfectly smooth main line track from one end of his section to the other with no dips or squiggles. The ideal track was one on which a passenger train would glide along at sixty or seventy miles an hour as smoothly as if on a dance floor. This ideal was seldom if ever achieved, but they all worked at it. A section gang would spend days raising and aligning a segment of track, and in just a few weeks the roadmaster, riding the last car of a passenger train would throw off a "butterfly" telling the foreman that the same bit of track rode like a washboard and asking why he hadn't fixed it already.[5]

If the track was out of alignment, the crew, equipped with aligning bars,[6] half on one rail and half on the other and all moving together, would heave the track to the left or right.[7] The foreman, positioned a rail length or so away, would gauge the move with his eye and then signal the crew to move ahead or back to the next spot that needed straightening.

Low spots in the track were raised with a track jack. The foreman would bend over the rail and sight along it. In response to his signal, two men would place the jack under the rail between the ties in the center of the low spot and jack the track up level, using an aligning bar as a jack handle. It usually took two men pumping that five-foot jack handle to raise the track. At the foreman's signal, one man would move the heavy jack forward or back to a new spot by sliding it on top of the rail while the other man carried the jack handle. They would repeat the operation until the entire segment was level. Then the crew would tamp ballast under the ties on the segment that had been raised.[8] If a train came along before the tamping was completed, it would be necessary to raise the track again.

In gravel ballast, tamping was done with shovels. In crushed rock, a tamping pick was used.[9] That first morning tamping ties, I was really giving that old pick a workout. I would straighten up each time I raised the pick and bring it down as hard as I could, occasionally knocking off the bottom corner of the tie. I was really working up a sweat. Tofanelli saw me and came running over.

"Stoppa work!" he ordered. "You gonna killa youself! You breaka the bottom of the tie, isa no good." He then had me go watch Clarence King, an old-time gandydancer and part-time section foreman, who showed me how to raise the pick just head high, without straightening up, and let it fall. He also showed me that by giving the pick a nudge with the knee as it was raised, the whole operation became much easier. "After all," he told me, smiling a little, "you've got to last out the day, and we've still got seven hours left."

He was right. That pick got awfully heavy before we broke for lunch, and it grew even heavier in the afternoon. It was a welcome break each time a train went by. As we were working on the eastbound track east of Tecoma, and the westbound track was a half mile to the north, we got only half the breaks we could have had if both tracks had been side by side.[10]

"If you can stick it out for three weeks, you'll have it made," I was told. Track labor was hard work. Not only physically taxing, but tedious. Raise that heavy pick, then drop it, raise it and drop it, over and over again. Switch to the other side of the rail and repeat the process, turn around and do the other side of the tie, then move to another tie, and start all over again.

There were occasional breaks in the routine. We spent part of one morning replacing a rail on the eastbound main line. With the new rail in place and the gauge spiking finished,[11] I picked up a spike maul and started to do my share of the spike driving. On the first swing, I put a half-moon dent in the top of that new rail. On the second one I broke the spike maul handle. I grabbed another spike maul and, on the next swing, broke the handle of that one. I hadn't yet touched the spike. Tofanelli came running over and gave me another job.

"You have to keep the handle dead level when you hit, or you break it every time," Clarence King told me. "John's worried we'll run out of handles, and the supply train isn't due for another two months."[12]

I had watched the section crews driving spikes for most of my life, and it looked so easy. Two-man teams working together in perfect harmony, taking exactly five blows to each spike, their mauls sparkling blurs in the sun. They were like a ballet—rhythmic, smooth, beautiful. But I couldn't do it. I had a lot to learn.

We spent several days in June on a work train reballasting the westbound main line. From Lucin to Tecoma, the westbound track snakes up a seven-mile-long hill, while the eastbound track runs straight down the hill from Tecoma to Lucin. In 1939 that westbound segment of main line may have been the only one on the Salt Lake Division that still had gravel ballast. The work train—consisting of an engine, several dump cars, a flanger car, and a caboose—moved slowly along the track dumping slag, which the railroad was trying out as ballast. The flanger leveled and smoothed the slag below the tops of the rails. Later we worked with an extra gang, raising the track and tamping the slag under the ties with power tampers running on compressed air.

The work train had to avoid other traffic, so we would work in spurts and then run to the nearest side track to wait for scheduled traffic to pass.

The work train was in the Montello yard one day, stopped alongside another train on an adjacent track. Our train was expected to move out at any moment, and I was standing in the center of a flatcar just ahead of the caboose. I could hear the cars jerking as the engine started, taking up the slack between the cars, and I braced myself, ready for the jolt to the car I was on. I could hear the sounds coming closer and closer, and just as my car picked up the slack, the train on the next track started up and I fell flat on the deck, to the vast amusement of the rest of the gang, who were watching from the caboose. I didn't think it was so funny—the deck of that flatcar was full of splinters.

On Independence Day I went to Lakeside for a visit. An excursion train from Ogden was in the yard, and Dad told me the roadmaster was on the train. On impulse, I climbed onto the train and, after searching several cars, I found him and asked for a transfer to Lakeside. He agreed and told me I would start working for Chet Davis on Monday.

Chet Davis was foreman of the Lakeside section, which extended from just west of Lakeside east across the Great Salt Lake nearly to the station at Midlake. Dad's section, Strongknob, ran west from the Lakeside section to some miles west of Hogup, an uninhabited siding. It was customary for the Lakeside and Strongknob gangs to work together. One day we might be changing a rail on the trestle out in the middle of the lake, and the next day could find us tamping ties out on the mud flat. Although I was not in Dad's gang, I might just as well have been. He took over my training as a gandydancer.

"Here's what I want you to do," he told me the first day we were tamping ties. "Set a pace you can keep up all day, and then don't you straighten up. Just keep right on working!"

He meant it. Nobody ever had reason to complain that he showed favoritism to his own boys. But he also showed me the little tricks that made some operations easier. For instance, one day as I was struggling to clear the ballast out from between two ties preparatory to replacing one of them, he showed me how, instead of fighting the rails, which were always in the way, to use the rails to increase the leverage on the shovel. "Let the rail work for you," he said.

At the end of three months, I was qualified as a full-fledged section laborer, and my pay was increased to the journeyman's scale—a one-cent raise to thirty-three cents an hour.

On August 12, at 9:33 P.M., the Southern Pacific's crack streamliner, the *City of San Francisco,* went off the rails in Palisade Canyon, sixteen miles west of Carlin, killing 24 people and injuring 121. Almost immediately there was talk of sabotage, and Dad and Chet Davis were concerned. We had left a number of tools alongside the track west of Lakeside, where we had been working that Saturday, and although it was far from likely that anyone with sabotage in mind would be out there on the mud flats, they decided to go out and pick up those tools. There were claw bars, wrenches, and spike mauls—tools that could be used to unspike, unbolt, and deflect a rail. So the next day, Sunday, Chet Davis, Dad, and I, with two other men, put a motorcar on the track and brought in those tools and locked them up. We didn't put in for overtime.

Although I had intended this narrative to cover only those years the Call family spent in Nevada, our stay in Lakeside, Utah, is important since my youngest brother, Lynn Bowen, was born in September 1939 while we were there. He wasn't really born at Lakeside. Two weeks before he was due, Mother went to Ogden and took up residence in a downtown hotel. When her time came, she went up to the Dee Hospital and gave birth with no members of the family around her for support. Dad went to her as soon as he could, but Lynn was born before he got there. A few days later, they brought Lynn to Lakeside and introduced him to the rest of us. It was strange having a tiny baby in the house, but we soon got used to it. Actually, he sort of took over the house. Everything seemed to revolve around his needs and wants. My sister Adona, who was thirteen, was especially enchanted by the whole thing.

In October, at the end of the busy season, as I had the least seniority on Chet Davis's gang, I was laid off. Except for Rey, the family spent the winter at Lakeside. Rey went to Salt Lake City and completed his freshman year at the University of Utah. As there was no school at Lakeside, none of the rest of the family went to school that winter.

25

Elwood

"I was the janitor as well as a student in the little school in Dublan, Mexico," Dad said. We were gathered in the "office" of our house in Lakeside. It was April 1, 1940, and Dad was reminiscing about some April Fool's pranks he had been involved in. Except for Rey, who was in Salt Lake City, we were all there, listening in astonishment as he told us of some of his escapades.

"It was my duty to ring the bell a half hour before school was to begin," he continued. "Then the teacher, Harrison Hurst, would ring it a second time when it was time for school to begin. The bell was in a belfry, with a rope hanging down through an opening about a foot and a half square. On this April Fool's Day, I rang the bell as usual and then tied a bucket of water on the floor above at the edge of the hole so that it would tip over when anyone pulled the bell rope. I then went home.

"On purpose I was a minute late for school, as I was afraid my face would give me away, and everyone would know who had done it. When I got to school, the teacher was completely soaked. Not only that, he had a bump on his head where the bucket had fallen through the hole and hit him. For years I didn't dare tell anyone who had pulled that stunt."

We were amazed. Our father did that? And this was only one of the escapades he told us about that evening. As a rule, he didn't talk much about his early life. We knew he had spent ten years in Mexico while growing up, and on several occasions he had told us about his exodus from Mexico just ahead of a band of "soldiers" who were bent on killing him and his companions, but this was a side of him we didn't suspect. He entertained us that evening with a number of stories about his early life, and years later, at our urging, he wrote them into his personal history.

Our father, Frank Elwood Call, was born August 19, 1892, in Bountiful, Utah, the fifth child and fourth son of Willard and Adelaide White Call. Willard's father was the noted Utah pioneer Anson Call, and Adelaide's father was John Stout White, a member of the historic Mormon Battalion. Elwood, as he was known in the family, wrote about his early life:

> I was named Frank after a friend of Mother and Father's—a Frenchman . . . whom my parents admired very much. . . .
>
> Too soon after my birth, my parents had the misfortune to lose my brother Jesse, next older than I, which may have caused [them] to be somewhat more protective of me. I seem to have led a very sheltered life . . . my earliest memory of it . . . goes back to when I wore a blue dress with white polka-dots. I must have been helping to paint the picket fence that surrounded our home in Bountiful, because the pretty blue dress had splotches of pinkish paint on it, the same color as the fence.
>
> I must have been three, or three-and-a-half or four, so why was I still wearing dresses? Was it because I looked, acted, or talked like a girl? Or was it that I just didn't have the guts to demand that I be dressed as a man should be dressed?[1]

He was known as Elwood until after he married and discovered that the rest of the world preferred people to use their first names. When Dad was about nine months old, his father was called to serve a mission for the Church of Jesus Christ of Latter-Day Saints. He went to England and was gone, by his own reckoning, twenty-five months and eleven days.[2]

"I don't remember his leaving," Dad wrote, "but I do remember his coming home. I had been two years or maybe a little more without a father in the home, and I resented this stranger." His account continues:

He took liberties with my mother, kissing and hugging her. He even presumed to tell me what I should do. Naturally, I resented his interfering with my personal liberty, so when he ordered me to come to prayer, I refused. He called me a second time, but I just stood in the corner saying, "I won't do it for you." I didn't object to prayer, I was accustomed to it, but to be taking orders from this stranger was just too much. However, I soon joined the family in prayer after a certain fleshy part of my anatomy had been warmed up.[3]

Dad, perhaps a bit overprotected due to the death of his older brother, tended to be something of a rebel in his early years. For instance:

The time came for me to go to school, and at first I thought it great fun. But after a while, the teacher began to get smart with me. She told me to copy words she had written on the blackboard, and she said I had to learn to spell and to read from a book. I made up my mind that if that was what they did at school, I'd had enough. Of course I knew Mother would not take the same view of the matter, so I decided not to tell her. I would just stay away, and no one would be the wiser.

My sister Rettie, and brothers Willard and Harold, went off to the school as usual, but I stayed down by the barn, meaning to keep out of sight. Mother soon saw me and urged me to go to school. I had had enough of school and didn't propose to go. Finally Mother started after me, I supposed to take me to school by the hand.

Going to school now looked more desirable than it had at first, so I decided I would do just that, but Mother had some idea of her own. I started as fast as I could run toward the schoolhouse, which was about six blocks from home, with Mother in hot pursuit. I thought I could easily outdistance Mother and get inside without being overtaken, but somehow she cut me off.

I then headed north across fields and irrigation ditches toward Uncle Israel's. Mother didn't falter. I led her through the roughest terrain I could find, hoping she would realize she couldn't overtake me and give up. Finally I drew near Uncle Israel's and Mother stopped to get her breath. Since I was no longer pursued, there was no longer reason for flight. I stopped and was soon busy playing with my cousins. Mother then played a sneaky trick on me.

When I was not looking, she grabbed me by the shirt collar and marched me off toward home. For three days she kept me in bed, entirely alone in the daytime. No company, no one to talk with—I just had to stay in bed. When at last she let me out, I was ready to go to school.[4]

On May 3, 1898, Father Willard enlisted in the army to fight in the Spanish-American War. He was assigned as a corporal to Battery A, Utah Light Artillery, and embarked in June for the Philippines. Arriving in Manila Bay in July, he took part in five battles and the bombardment of Manila, was discharged early in December, and arrived home by way of Nagasaki on January 18, 1899. He had been away just over eight months.[5]

Meanwhile, Dad's childish escapades continued, but occasionally he was victim rather than perpetrator:

> I suppose many brothers play dirty little tricks on their younger brothers. My eldest brother [Willard] was no exception. One day he asked me if I wanted a live bird. Of course I did, so he told me to go to the hollow below the barn and there I would find his hat lying on the ground. I was to lift it carefully, slip my hand under, palm down, and grab.
>
> I did as I was told, and what I grabbed could not be called a bird by any stretch of the imagination. After I stomped his hat in it, I had far less trouble washing my hand than he had washing his hat.[6]

Soon after Father Willard's military career ended, he made a trip to visit his brother, Anson Bowen, in Colonia Dublan, Chihuahua, Mexico. Following his return to Bountiful, he decided to move his family to Mexico, and on June 9, 1902, they left Bountiful.[7] It was in Mexico that Dad was introduced to the Spanish language. Although the Mormons in the Colonies had their own schools, studying Spanish appeared to be a requirement. He was able to practice the language by clerking in his father's store in Dublan, and later, when he became manager of the commissary at the Hacienda Marquesote, some sixty miles north of Dublan, he increased his use and understanding of the language. This resulted in some confusion among the native Mexicans, since he sounded like one of them but looked like an "Anglo," a "norteamericano."

The revolution, referred to by the Mormon colonists as "The Troubles," began far to the south and in the Colonies consisted at first merely of rumors—disquieting, but nothing to be concerned about as long as the fighting didn't move north. But it did. Armed gangs of men would appear and demand all sorts of things, especially horses and saddles. Soon there were no saddle horses or saddles left in town.

Then one day General José Inez Salazar rode into town with a small detachment of soldiers and demanded all of the colonists' weapons. Runners were sent throughout the community requesting that all guns be turned in. The colonists complied, but they had quietly brought in about seventy new 30-30 rifles with ammunition, and as these were well hidden, they were not surrendered.

About a week later, sometime in May or June 1912, they were ordered to board a train and leave Mexico. Each family was allowed to take only one suitcase and one roll of bedding. As Dad later commented:

> We saw no reason for our expulsion, and at first we thought that in a few days or weeks at the most we would be back, comfortably located in our own homes. We had broken no laws. We were a tax-paying, law-abiding people who added greatly to the economy of the state of Chihuahua. Perhaps the best reason we should have stayed was the reason we were expelled: We were prosperous. . . .
>
> It was not an easy matter to leave our homes in Mexico. Some of the colonists had lived there thirty years and considered it their permanent home. Some had even become naturalized Mexican citizens. Most families left some loved one buried in Mexican soil. We left a tiny baby, Afton, Mother's fourteenth, only fifteen days old when she died.[8]

Except for Dad, his older brother Harold, and a few other young men who were left to water the animals and do other chores, the entire community of about twelve hundred souls left on the train. There were not enough coaches, and the Call family climbed into a boxcar. Shortly after they left, the railroad stopped operating.

A few days later, the colonists were warned of a plot to kill all those remaining, and they gathered at the tithing office at 6:00 the next morning, ready to leave. They had the new rifles with them, but the only means of transportation was the few remaining workhorses. All the saddle horses and saddles had already been taken by various Mexican fighting groups. They left early in the morning, riding west to the nearby mountains, where they were to meet similar groups from other colonies. Dad was riding a mare with a crooked foot, and he used a blanket in lieu of a saddle. He describes the exodus thus:

> We forded the river, and about a mile beyond we came upon a small detachment of troops. They were completely surprised; in fact, I think they

were asleep until the head of our column arrived. They made no effort to stop us, but they followed us, apparently thinking we were unarmed. . . .

We succeeded in getting among the hills before they came in range of their guns. They stopped, dismounted, and fired at us. We kept right on going as fast as we could on work horses, but soon the Mexicans came in range again and fired another volley in our direction. They were probably riding our good saddle horses, and we knew that we could not outdistance them.

They kept firing at us until Willie Smith was hit in the leg by a spent ball. His injury was not serious, but Bishop Thurbur decided it was time to stop the sniping. He detailed three of our young men who were expert shots to wait until our pursuers dismounted again for another shot at us, and then to drop a few shots among them, but above all not to hit anyone. "Just kick up the dust so they will know we are armed." This worked, for we were no longer pursued.[9]

The rendezvous point was a small box canyon, where they joined other similar groups. They had ridden all day without food and with little water. Someone had brought a sack of flour and a side of bacon, but no one had brought anything to cook food in. The flour and bacon were divided up, and each group was left to do what they could with what they had.

Our group gouged out a small hole in the ground about the size of a mixing bowl. Into this we pressed Harold's raincoat to form a bowl. In this we mixed flour and water into a dough without baking powder or other leavening. We cut willows from the edge of a nearby brook and wrapped strips of dough and strips of bacon around the end of the willow which we held over a fire until it was partially cooked. This was not the best meal I had ever eaten, but after an all-day ride with no breakfast and no lunch, it didn't taste bad at all.[10]

When all the men from the other settlements arrived, they headed in a single group north for the U.S. border, a daylong trip that was accomplished without incident. This group of several hundred men and boys arrived, sore and dirty, in Hachita, New Mexico, and from there secured train passage to El Paso, where they were united with their families. Dad accompanied his family on their return to Bountiful. They arrived in the summer of 1912, having been gone ten years. They had left everything they owned in Mexico. Dad was now twenty years old.

“I may well be the only survivor of that ride from Dublan to the U.S. border,” he wrote many years later. “I have kept track as best I could, and one by one they have passed away. This makes me feel old and somewhat sad.”[11]

Dad worked at a few odd jobs around Bountiful and then got a job as a track laborer on the Oregon Short Line, which later became a part of the Union Pacific System. He worked for a man named Joe Hancock. He had been on the job only a few months when his cousin Willey phoned and told him he had gotten him a job at the State School for the Deaf and Blind in Ogden. Dad didn’t even bother to tell anyone on the railroad that he was quitting.

A few days after he had left for Ogden, Mr. Hancock showed up looking for him. When he was told that Dad had quit, he expressed his regrets and informed Father Willard that he had been planning to make a track foreman of his son.

Elwood started to work in the kitchen at the school in February 1913 at thirty dollars a month with board and room. Later he was offered the position of stationary fireman at the heating plant, and his pay was raised to forty dollars. It was his practice to keep five dollars out of his pay and send the rest home to Mother Adelaide to help the family. Out of what he kept, he would occasionally take one of the girls who worked at the school to a movie, but he had to be careful—admission cost ten cents.

In September 1913, a little Danish immigrant girl started working in the laundry at the school. Her name was Johanne, but everyone called her Yonna. Elwood didn’t pay much attention to her at first except to tease her—it seemed that he teased all the girls at one time or another. She didn’t like him.

“Du er en gammel gedebuk!” she told him. “You are an old billy goat!” It was the worst thing she could think of. He had a good ear for languages, and he remembered what she had said long enough to find someone to translate it for him.

Another time she told him, “You are the one person here I could hate.” He later wrote: “I don’t now know by what mental processes things began to change or what quirks in my disposition caused me to turn toward her. I must have reasoned that if she could hate she could also love. . . . I was not mistaken. She could love, really love with a devotion I was not then able to understand.”[12]

They were married December 13, 1916, and in January 1917 he was called to labor in the Spanish American Mission. He spent the next two and a half years in Colorado and New Mexico, improving his Spanish as he worked to convert descendants of people who had lived in the area two hundred years before there was a United States of America. Mother stayed home and supported him in every way she could.

Back home in Ogden, Dad and his young bride began raising a family. They went to Butte, Montana, to join Father Willard in selling woolen goods; then Dad got a job selling a new type of broom with black fibers instead of broom corn. He was selling brooms in Butte when I was born. Later we moved to Missoula, and were on our way to California to continue the broom business when Mother became ill with erysipelas. We had stopped in Salt Lake City for a visit, intending to stay only a few days. It took months for her to recover, and the move to California was abandoned.

Back in Ogden, Dad went back to his old job at the School for the Deaf and was appointed as a counselor to the president of the LDS Branch for the Deaf, where he became fluent in American Sign Language. Later he tried selling life insurance, with rather indifferent results. Finally he got a job as a salesman for the L. H. Manning Company, which operated a series of commissaries along the Southern Pacific between Ogden and Reno.

One of the foremen he did business with was Jess Higley at Moor, Nevada. Jess persuaded him to come to work and told him that in just a few months he too could be a section foreman. So fifteen years after he quit his job as a gandydancer for the Oregon Short Line, he started over again, this time on the Southern Pacific.

26

Foreman

"I want you to let those men go," the roadmaster commanded, nodding toward the two black men who worked for Dad. "I don't want any of those fellows in my district! I'll send you two men to replace them."

"Absolutely not," Dad countered. "They're good men. They do good work, and they work hard. They will stay as long as I have work for them."

The roadmaster glared at him and then climbed onto his little Fairmont motorcar and sat in stony silence while his driver started the car and they moved off up the track toward Winnemucca. The roadmaster was new and was busy reworking his district to his own liking. The black men had been hired by the previous roadmaster and sent to work for Dad, who was now foreman of the section at Imlay, Nevada. Dad was not getting off to a good start with his new boss.

The time was early 1948, before anyone on the railroad ever heard about civil rights, and there would have been no trouble for anyone if Dad had complied with the roadmaster's wishes. The men stayed, and the roadmaster decided not to push it, but the friction didn't stop there.

One day the roadmaster was bossing a work train with the Imlay crew on board. Something happened that he thought was Dad's fault, and with typical railroad profanity he started to reprimand him. While he was carrying on, Dad took the man by the elbow, guided him aside where no one else could hear, and then quietly let him understand that he had no intention of taking that kind of abuse.

"If I've done something wrong, I'll take your correction. But I don't use that kind of language, and I won't have it directed at me."

The roadmaster got the message, but didn't like him any better for it, and after a few more incidents Dad was beginning to look for an available section in another roadmaster's district. However, as they continued to work together, they began to regard each other with a grudging respect, and finally they may even have gotten to be pretty good friends.

Although he displayed an outgoing love for his fellow men, Dad was not universally loved in return. But he had the respect of all who knew him. How could it be any other way? He always treated everyone he knew, including the men working for him, with consideration and respect, and he was scrupulously fair with both the company and his men.

His section crews always arrived early enough to have the motorcar on the track and loaded, and when Dad, looking at his watch, gave the signal, they would climb on the motorcar and be on their way on the dot at 7:00 A.M. In the afternoons, he would try to time his arrival back at the toolhouse to allow just enough time to get the motorcar off the track, put the tools away, and then lock up at exactly 3:30. When train traffic forced them to come in early to avoid being late, his crews would sort scrap, cut weeds, or do other useful work until quitting time.

Dad's tenure as foreman at Strongknob lasted three years. Then in late 1942 or early 1943, tired of staying at Lakeside by himself while his wife and family—those not in military service—spent the school year in town, he took a job as assistant foreman in the Ogden rail yard.

Due to the war, rail traffic was extremely heavy, roadbeds were beginning to deteriorate, and it was hard to find healthy young men to work on the railroad—they were all in the armed services. Rey, Grant, Dale, and I were all in the service, and my sister Adona was working in the rail yard as a supply clerk.

Desperate for labor, the railroad decided to recruit men from Mexico, who were allowed to enter the country with temporary work permits. Because of his knowledge of Spanish, Dad was appointed to do the recruiting, and a job was created for him. As "labor inspector," he would travel to Los Angeles, San Diego, or the border, recruit a carload of men, escort them to Nevada, and distribute them along the railroad where help was needed. In the event any of the men got into trouble and had to be deported, he was the one who escorted them back to the border.

With the return of servicemen after the war and a plentiful labor supply, the job of labor inspector was eliminated. Dad was then offered a position as general foreman of extra gangs. Not only would this bring him more pay, but he would be in line for further promotion. It was from the ranks of general foremen that roadmasters were frequently appointed. But this would also have meant periods of separation from his family, and he had already had too many years of that sort of life, so he declined.

The section at Imlay came open, and Dad successfully bid the job. By the time he got to Imlay in June 1947, his household had shrunk to three—he, my mother, and my youngest brother Lynn, who was now nearly eight. Dad's three oldest sons—Rey, Grant, and I—were married, and the rest didn't want to make the move. Later in the year, when Dale married, Cyril went to Imlay, where he stayed until he left to serve in the Spanish American LDS Mission, the same one Dad had labored in more than thirty years earlier.

In April 1948, my sister Adona married, and Mother realized a long-held dream. She went to Denmark for a three-month visit, leaving the care of her home and husband to my sister, whose new husband, Eugene, worked on the section for Dad.

On her return, Mother summed up her trip: "I enjoyed the visit. It was good to visit relatives and old friends. But now I have had enough of Denmark and the Danes—they're just a bunch of foreigners, and I don't want to go back!"

Shortly after he arrived home from his mission, my brother Cyril married Joanne, a girl he had gone to school with in Ogden. The only one of the children left at home now was Lynn. In 1956, Dad successfully bid the foreman's job at Carlin, where they remained until he retired from the railroad late in 1958.

Together with my wife and me, Dad and Mother bought a small fruit farm in Perry, Utah, and built a home on it by mating an old motel unit to a small house trailer. Lynn attended Brigham Young University and then was called on an LDS mission. After serving two years in California, he returned to BYU. The last of the Call children, he was married in 1963 and was awarded a bachelor's degree from BYU in 1964.[1]

Dad and Mother spent their last years in Perry. Dad retired with no regrets and said he didn't miss the railroad at all. Dad helped my children work in the orchard, and every year he planted and took loving care of a small garden. Except for occasional trips to Mexico or to California to visit their children and grandchildren living there, they were content to stay at home in their little house. They were affectionately known throughout Perry as Grandpa and Grandma Call.

"I've never had a job of importance. Never had money above bare subsistence," he wrote in 1963. But to anyone interested he would confide, "We have all we want and need right here. We want for nothing. Can anyone be richer than that?"

In 1965, Dad and Mother's children gave them tickets on an excursion flight to Denmark. Mother changed her mind about not going back to Denmark, and Dad began brushing up on his Danish, which he hadn't had much chance to use for more than thirty years.

They were gone a month and had a wonderful time. Mother's relatives embraced Dad as a long-lost cousin. They traveled throughout the country and even went to the famous Fourth of July celebration in Northern Jutland. "After all," Dad said, "the king and queen were there, so we thought we might as well go."

Dad must have gotten fairly comfortable with the Danish language. In one of the cities they visited, they stopped to ask directions from a police officer. Dad walked right up and asked the questions, then turned to Mother and began to translate what the officer had said, much as he did when they were in Mexico.

Suddenly he stopped, looking a bit foolish: "Well, you heard him." Mother just smiled sweetly and took his arm.

In the late 1970s Mother's health began to fail. Since her recurring bouts with erysipelas in 1920, she had never been robust, always seemed to catch cold easily, and tired readily. Yet she never let these things stop her from doing what she thought she had to do, and she never complained. She began to spend much of her time in a wheelchair, and Dad spent his days taking care of her.

At about 7:00 A.M. on June 12, 1980, Dad called my wife, Delilah, and told her he thought he was having a heart attack. We lived just a few hundred yards from their small home, and she rushed up to see what she could do. When she got there, the screen door was locked. She called to Dad that she couldn't get in, and then watched him as he struggled to get to his feet, cross the room, and open the door.

A call to Dad's doctor produced an ambulance, and he was rushed to the hospital. Once there, he fretted about leaving Mother alone; however, he seemed to be doing well, and no one was worried. But suddenly, late in the afternoon, he had a massive heart attack and died. He was eighty-seven.

Thereafter Mother lived alone in their little house and liked it that way. I would visit her at least once each day, and Delilah would look in on her frequently. A nurse from the county came twice a week and bathed her, and my brothers and sister from Ogden were frequent visitors. After about a year and a half, it was apparent that she couldn't continue to live by herself.

All her children were anxious to have her come and live with them, but she refused at first. She finally consented to live with my wife and me, but only because we were closest to her home, and she was determined to move back "as soon as I get to feeling better."

Her health continued to deteriorate until she was almost completely confined to her bed. She was never cross, never complained, smiling sweetly at those who helped her. At about 11:00 in the evening on November 17, 1982, I went up to bed, and Delilah decided to look in on Mother once more before she too retired.

"Wendell," she called, "I think your mother has gone." It was true. She had quietly slipped away in her sleep sometime between 10:00 and 11:00. She was ninety-one.

It has been said that some marriages are made in heaven. If that is true, the union between my father, Frank Elwood Call, and my mother, Johanne Oline Schantz Jorgensen, surely was one of them.

Notes

Chapter 1. Moor

1. *Stationary fireman:* The person who keeps the furnace for the boilers stoked.

2. *Gandydancer,* also *gandy dancer:* The term comes from the Gandy Manufacturing Company of Chicago, which formerly made many of the tools used by section gangs. See Ramon F. Adams, *The Language of the Railroader* (Norman: University of Oklahoma Press, 1977), 66. A section gang tamping ballast under the ties with shovels gave the appearance of performing an odd sort of dance.

3. The tunnel no longer exists, and all but two of the original ten passenger train tracks have disappeared.

4. Also called a *news butch* or *candy butch* (Adams, *Language of the Railroader,* 104).

5. In laying track, great effort was made to keep the roadbed as level as possible. Low hills were "cut" through, and the removed materials were used to build up the grades between hills.

6. A 4-8-2 Mountain-type engine with seventy-three-inch driving wheels. On the Southern Pacific, the serial numbers of these engines were assigned in the 43XX series; therefore, as a class they were referred to as "4300s." See Lynn H. Westcott, *Steam Locomotives* (Waukesha, Wisc.: Kalmbach, 1960), 177.

7. Officially, the locomotive was called an *engine.* Other terms used were *pig,* or *pig iron*—but never *loco,* which is a term used by model railroaders and their suppliers. I have, however, heard railroaders on the SP use the term in its Spanish sense, that is, to describe someone who was not quite right in the head.

Chapter 2. The Tie House

1. The *road engine,* the engine coupled directly to the head end of the train, was the main line engine assigned to pull the train. The helper engines were coupled on at the bottom of a hill and uncoupled when the train reached the top.

2. A Y-shaped section of track used to turn engines around where there was no turntable.

Chapter 3. One-Room School

1. This arrangement was not at all uncommon for those railroad families who could afford to maintain two households. I have often thought that such an arrangement must have been difficult for the employees who had to spend weeks and months alone in tiny, isolated places like Moor.

2. *Shoofly:* A temporary track, usually built around an obstacle such as a wreck, but in this case constructed merely to set out a car without tying up usable track. To build a shoofly, rails were spiked to ties laid without ballast on more or less level ground. Then a set of main line or side track rails was unbolted and partially unspiked, and bent to connect to the ends of the shoofly rails. With these rails bolted and spiked in place, the shoofly was ready to be used—very carefully!

Chapter 4. Cabin Fever

1. *Partridge's Dictionary of Slang and Unconventional English* (New York: Macmillan, 1989) defines *cabin fever* as a state of being mentally unbalanced or crazy. No one at Moor suffered to that extent—we were just plain tired of being shut in day after day.

2. The builders of the original transcontinental railroad had been concerned with laying as many miles of track as quickly as possible. It was often cheaper and faster to go around an object than over it or through it. Later, when they found themselves in the transportation business, they rerouted a number of miles of track in Utah and Nevada to cut out curves, shorten distances, and save on operating costs.

3. Before centralized traffic control was installed, safe distances between trains were maintained by *block signals.* Properly called *semaphores,* these were tall towers with arms that moved up and down to signal to approaching trains whether or not the next "block," or segment of track, was clear. At night, red and green lights indicated the status of the blocks.

If a signal arm was in the up position or the light showed red, the engineer was supposed to stop his train until the block cleared—that is, if the train in the block ahead was traveling in the same direction. On single track with traffic running in both directions, things were more complicated. Where two trains were headed toward each other on single track, the inferior train was directed by the train dispatcher to wait on a side track ("go in the hole") until the superior train had passed and the block cleared.

The train dispatcher had no way of communicating directly with any train crew. Instructions were given by telegraph or telephone to operators at OS (pronounced "oh-ess" from the words "on schedule") stations at intervals along the way, who relayed the dispatcher's instructions to the passing train crews by means of message hoops—one for the engineer and one for the conductor. Moor was an OS station, and the little depot was manned around the clock, seven days a week.

4. On some roads, the term *speeder* referred to what we on the SP called a *motorcar* (Adams, *Language of the Railroader,* 102).

5. They had probably had such a plan in mind before they left Moor. If they had taken us along, we would all have had to walk the whole nine miles back up the hill.

6. *Motorcars* were furnished in three sizes. The smallest, with room for one or two riders, were used by signal maintainers and occasionally by roadmasters. Most of these were propelled by single-cylinder gasoline engines. The midsize motorcars had room for six or eight riders and were capable of pulling (or pushing) a small trailer called a "pushcar." These motorcars were used by section gangs and were propelled by two-cylinder engines. The largest motorcars, capable of pulling three or four trailers loaded with men and equipment, were used by the large extra gangs. These motorcars were equipped with four-cylinder Model T engines.

Motorcars had to be light enough for the crews to "throw" them on and off the track easily. Like most railroad equipment, motorcars were designed to run equally well in either direction. On the earliest motorcars the engine was geared (or drive-chained) directly to the driving wheels, and the cars had to be pushed to get the engine started. As there was no clutch, the engine stopped when the car stopped. Later models were equipped with hand cranks or self-starters and clutches so they could be shifted to run in either direction.

As motorcars were not supposed to compete with trains, the wheel axles of motorcars were insulated so they would not affect block signals. Thus, train crews had no way of knowing, for instance, if a motorcar was on the main line track just around the next curve—nor was it their responsibility to know. It was up to the foreman or other person operating the motorcar to avoid the trains; getting his motorcar hit was a sure way for a foreman or a signal maintainer to lose his job.

7. I never really knew the location of the spring. For years I assumed the marshy place covered by standing water on the flat just below the pump house was the spring, but I know now that that was just the overflow from the pumping operation.

Chapter 5. Grant's Mountain

1. *Railroad torpedo:* A detonating device fastened to the top of a rail and exploded by the pressure of a locomotive or car passing over it, to give an audible signal to members of the locomotive crew. A torpedo was flat, approximately two inches square, with an explosive charge in the center. To hold the torpedo on the rail, a flat metal strip extended from each of three sides. The strips opposite each other were bent to hold the torpedo on the rail. The third strip extended along the top of the rail in the direction of the expected traffic. When the steel wheel of a train rolled over the torpedo, it exploded with a loud report.

Two torpedoes were a caution signal; one torpedo meant stop. To protect the rear end of a train stopped on the main line, the rear brakeman (also called the *rear shack, hind shack,* or *rear flag*), carrying a red flag or red signal lantern and a supply of torpedoes, walked back from the train a distance of up to a mile (depending on the terrain, the visibility, the rule book, and what he thought he could get away with). He would then place two torpedoes on the right rail at a distance of two rail lengths. Returning to about half the distance from the stopped train, he would place one torpedo on the rail, and he would then stand there with his red flag or red signal lantern until called in.

When called in by the engineer (five blasts of the whistle to call a flagman in from east or north, four from west or south), he would pick up the single torpedo and return to the train. The two torpedoes he had placed farther back were left as a warning to the engineer of any following train. If the rear brakeman were inadvertently to leave the single torpedo, the engineer of the following train—even if passing through hours later—would have no choice but to bring his train to a complete stop and then "flag through the block," that is, have the head brakeman walk ahead with a red flag or lantern until the next block signal, indicating a clear track ahead, could be seen.

2. *Fusees* were another element of the railroad signaling equipment. A red fusee burning beside the track signaled an approaching engineer to stop his train. When the brakeman who was flagging to the rear of a train was called in, he would pick up his single torpedo and then "spike a torch," that is, light a fusee and drop it to stick upright on the end of a tie. As long as the fusee burned (ten or fifteen minutes), any following train was required to stop. Later, fusees were made without spikes, since a fusee occasionally set the tie to which it was spiked on fire. The spikeless fusees were to be dropped on the ballast off the end of the tie. I have heard that some roads used fusees in several colors, but red was the only color I saw on the SP.

3. Cheaper watches were available, many with a representation of a steam engine engraved (or stamped) on the back of the case to fool unwary buyers into thinking they had railroad watches. Most of these watches were of the stem-set variety. Due to the possibility of the stem catching on something, pulling out to the reset position, and accidentally resetting the time, stem-set watches were prohibited for railroad use.

The back of Dad's watch was plain, as were those of all the railroad men's watches I ever saw. In addition to each railroad man checking his watch frequently against a standard timepiece (or by telephone), the railroad employed a "watch inspector," who checked each employee's watch at regular intervals. Watches also required regular cleaning and servicing by an approved watch repairman who would furnish a "loaner" while the owner's watch was in his shop.

4. We called them "Mexicans." They proudly called themselves "Mexicans" or in Spanish, "Mexicanos," or "La Gente Mexicana."

Chapter 7. Learning to Swim in the Desert

1. Dale L. Morgan, *The Humboldt: Highroad of the West* (New York: Rinehart, 1943), 5.

Chapter 8. Shoshone

1. And maybe Bill Mahoney did own it all. At the time this incident took place, each school district was autonomous and virtually independent. Any community with five or more children of school age could organize a school district, hire teachers, and then draw funds from the state to operate the school under the authority of the state superintendent of public instruction.

The state employed deputy superintendents to supervise each school. E. E. Franklin, for instance, was responsible for all the schools in Elko County, while Florence Peacocke was responsible for the schools in Humboldt, Pershing, Eureka, and Lander Counties. (Teachers were understandably nervous just prior to and during the deputy superintendents' visits, and of course this nervousness was transmitted to the children.)

2. Shoshone Point was the northern extremity of the Shoshone Range. From Beowawe, the river and the two railroads run nearly due north until they round the end of the range at Shoshone Point, where they turn west.

Chapter 11. Cutting Costs and Other Moves

1. I think it was Mr. House who was there in the depot in Elko that night, but it may have been someone else. I remember that it was a railroad man somewhat older than Dad who was very boisterous in congratulating Dad on his new job.

2. Actually, the segment defined as *Joint Operations* lay between Alazon, four miles west of Wells, and Weso, four miles east of Winnemucca. The Joint Operations segment, comprising nearly 280 miles of main line, incidentally made for some rather strange railroading. The westbound and eastbound tracks were miles apart over much of the distance. Residents of Battle Mountain, for instance, had to go to North Battle Mountain, a distance of four miles, to board an eastbound train. To catch the same train, residents of Shoshone had to go to Dunphy, a walk (usually) of about two miles.

3. The *engineer,* also called a *hog head* or *hogger* (Adams, *Language of the Railroader,* 55).

Chapter 12. Dan

1. Robert M. Hanft, *Red River: Paul Bunyan's Own Lumber Company and Its Railroads* (Chico: California State University, 1980), 23.

2. Ibid., 54.

3. Telegraph receivers were mounted in an open wooden box with sloping sides on the end of a jointed swing arm, which could be brought close to the operator when in use and then pushed out of the way. The box acted in part as a resonator for the receiver, but in most telegraph offices the sound was usually amplified further by means of a Prince Albert tobacco can tucked between the receiver and the back of the box.

4. *Bug:* A telegraph-sending instrument. Many operators, including George Gale, preferred a type of instrument with a key mounted to work from side-to-side, pushed one way for dots and the other way for dashes. These instruments were not furnished by the companies but were owned by the operators themselves. An experienced operator receiving a message could not only tell if one of these special keys were being used but also recognize the *fist* of the sender. An operator's fist, or the way in which he operated his instrument, was as personal as his signature and as easily recognized.

5. Jess Higley habitually wore riding pants and high-laced boots at work. Except when they went to church, Odell and Blain wore them as well. Dad also wore them, at least at the beginning of his railroad career. Rey and I had asked for riding pants and boots, too, but it wasn't until the autumn of 1931 that Mother and Dad were able to buy them for us. For winter, new sheepskin coats and imitation-leather aviator's helmets completed our outfits.

6. Of course, the cowboys didn't hang around the school to make a nuisance of themselves, but when invitations went out to attend our Halloween or Christmas programs, they all showed up.

Chapter 13. Elsie

1. *Eureka Sentinel,* January 30; February 6, 13, 20, and 27; March 5 and 12, 1932, p. 1.

Chapter 14. Death of a Way Station

1. *Spot a car:* To place a car in a designated place (Adams, *Language of the Railroader,* 144).

2. As Charlie Helton was not renowned for telling the truth, Dad expressed the opinion that Charlie may have just "squatted" there.

3. They were hand pumps, the kind that had a ten-gallon, graduated glass cylinder at the top. The attendant worked the handle of a hand pump back and forth to fill the cylinder, then gauged the amount of gasoline dispensed using the marks on the glass.

Chapter 17. "But What Did You Do for Entertainment?"

1. No. 6 dry cells looked like oversize flashlight batteries. They were about three inches in diameter and six inches long, and each cell produced 1.5 volts.

2. Years later she told us that the "Fatty Lamb" story had appeared in her first reader, supplied by her school in Denmark. Today's educators would have been horrified.

3. The most memorable thing about Reverend Schriver was his habit of offering long prayers. For him, ten minutes was a short prayer, and twenty minutes was not unusual.

Chapter 18. Summer Fun—and Work

1. The first trick operator, who also held the title of station agent, was the most senior of the group and worked from 8:00 A.M. until 4:00 P.M. The second trick operator, next in seniority, worked the shift from 4:00 P.M. until 12:00 midnight. Mrs. Lewis had bid on the job knowing that it would be a permanent assignment. They did not rotate shifts.

Chapter 19. A New School

1. Cinnabar, we learned, is mercury ore (mercuric sulfide, HgS).

2. The annual report for the Beowawe School District for the year ending June 30, 1934, shows school beginning October 2, 1933, and ending June 8, 1934, for a total of 170 days (*Annual Report of Beowawe School District, Eureka County, Nevada, for the Year Ending June 30, 1934,* Nevada State Library and Archives, Carson City). The report shows 20 school days from April 16 through May 11 and 20 days from May 14 through June 8. No Saturday school days were reported.

3. The correct term, of course, is *hillside,* but most people I knew called it a *side hill.* There were yarns about the "side hill dodger," an animal with legs shorter on one side than the other. It was said that if a left-handed side hill dodger met a right-handed one, neither one would give up the right-of-way. They would stand there nose-to-nose until they starved to death.

Chapter 20. Montello

1. Everyone in town called it the *roundhouse,* but it wasn't round—it was rectangular. In larger yards, where the number of engines to be housed warranted it, the engine shed was round, or rather built in the shape of an arc, with the track from each stall converging on a turntable, which was used to turn the engines around or direct them onto the proper track.

2. Railroaders used a language of their own, a colorful jargon that varied from road to road in different parts of the country. For instance, the company hotel in Montello was called the *beanery.* A beanery, in the language of the railroader, is a railroad eating house. In this case, the entire building, hotel and café, was called the beanery, even after the café had been eliminated. Other words used by the railroaders were as follows:

Engineer: A person employed to run a locomotive; also called *hog head, hogger, hog jockey, hog mauler.*

Fireman: One whose duty it was to keep up steam. The old method was by shoveling coal, but all the SP engines were oil burners; also called *bake head, smoke agent, tallow pot.*

Hostler: One whose job it was to move engines in and out of the roundhouse and also to fire up the engines.

Boilermaker: A person who assembled or repaired boilers (not to be confused with whiskey with a beer chaser).

Car knocker: A car inspector or car repairman; also called *car tink, car toad, car whacker.*

Machinist: A highly skilled employee who repaired and rebuilt engines and other machinery. Machinists prided themselves on their ability not only to replace a worn part but also, if need be, to make a new one. It was said that some of them could actually manufacture a locomotive from the ground up.

Mechanic: An employee who repaired everything. Under this heading were grouped the separate classes or trades, such as *boilermakers, car knockers, and machinists.*

Yardmaster: The man in charge of all operations in a rail yard, including moving and setting out cars and making up trains; also called *bull goose, dinger, ringmaster, yardman.*

Signalman: There were two classes of signalmen: those who were part of a traveling *signal gang* and performed heavy installation and repairs on signal equipment, and *signal maintainers,* who were permanently stationed to maintain such equipment within an assigned length of main line or area of a rail yard.

Switchman: Also called a *switch monkey,* a worker who operated a switch to turn an engine or train from one track to another. Although brakemen, section foremen, yardmasters, and others who had switchlock keys also "threw" switches, the switchman's sole job was running from switch to switch in a rail yard to control movement of engines or trains. (As a rule, yard switches were not locked. For safety reasons, locks were required on main line switches, that is, any switch capable of diverting a train from the main line. The reason for the lock is obvious. An open switch in the path of a train approaching at full speed would likely "put it in the ditch." For simplicity, all the switchlocks were identical. A single key would open every switchlock on the division.)

Telegrapher: Although proficiency in Morse code was a requirement, most of the communication necessary to control the trains was done by telephone; also called *brass pounder, buzzer, sparks,* or just *operator.*

Extra gang: On the SP, extra gangs were mobile maintenance crews living in converted boxcars that could be moved from place to place as their services were needed. Extra gangs did the really heavy work, such as replacing or laying several miles of new rails. A rail-laying gang was called a *steel gang.* Other specialties were:

B&B gang: The *bridge and building gang,* as the name implies, constructed or repaired bridges and buildings. These gangs were usually fairly large, employing twenty to thirty men.

Door knob gang: The door knob gang was a two-man B&B gang employed to perform minor repairs and maintenance of buildings, such as painting or replaçing windows.

Signal gang: This group made major repairs to or replaced railroad signal equipment.

I have listed here those terms I remember as commonly used on the Salt Lake Division of the Southern Pacific. These and other terms meaning the same things were used on other roads (Adams, *Language of the Railroader,* 11).

Chapter 21. Lee Martin

1. *Montello Consolidated Schools* was not the original name. The name was assumed in 1937 when the school absorbed one or two smaller school districts nearby and the expanded district began busing the children to Montello. This also allowed the Montello district to hire more teachers and expand the curriculum. Beginning in 1938, Lee Martin, the principal, taught only Spanish while Miss Myna Turner taught the commercial subjects. Miss Berneice Blakely taught music and English, and George W. Tharp, who had replaced Coach Weaver in 1937, taught science, P. E., math, and history. Noble Revier Palmer taught math, mechanical drawing, and manual training. (See *Appendix to Journals of Senate and Assembly of the Thirty-Ninth Session of the Legislature of the State of Nevada, 1939,* Volume II: *State of Nevada Educational Directory and Information as to Certification of Teachers and Retirement Salaries,* November 1938, p. 20.)

2. My class of 1938 could have held our reunions in a telephone booth if we had ever had any. The class roll: Norma Sanders, Lawrence Richards, and F. Wendell Call.

3. I heard Mr. Martin give that little speech after I started school in Montello. I got the impression that he had given it before.

4. Veterans Administration records for Leland Stanford Martin (VA Form 10-P-10, *Application for Hospital Treatment or Domiciliary Care,* December 22, 1969) list his mother's maiden name as Mary J. Carmen. Her death certificate, No. 69-002156, issued by the state of Nevada, lists her father's name as Jake Cameron.

5. In frontier societies, it appears that males have always outnumbered females, and although Nevada in the 1930s was hardly a frontier, there were more men than women in every community we lived in. But among the children of those communities there were nearly always more boys than girls. I can offer no explanation, but here is the way it was:

Holborn School at Moor, 1928–30	4 boys, 2 girls
Dunphy School at Shoshone, 1930–31	3 boys, 2 girls
Dunphy School at Dunphy, 1931–32	5 boys, 5 girls
Beowawe School, 1932–33	34 boys, 14 girls

Beowawe School, 1933–34	33 boys, 16 girls
Montello High School, 1932–38	44 boys, 35 girls

6. It was customary to charge men and boys admission to a dance, usually a dollar. Women and girls were admitted free since there were fewer females than males in almost every community. Mixing at a dance was expected, and a man or boy who brought a date was entitled by custom to the first and last dances with her. For the rest, he took his chances. For formal dances like the Junior Prom, dance programs were issued to each guest, and the more popular girls had their programs completely filled in within the first half hour.

Chapter 22. Crickets

1. *Works Progress Administration:* One of the government organizations set up to bring the country out of the depression, the WPA put the unemployed to work on a variety of public works projects.

2. A dense mass of crickets was referred to as a "swarm," a "herd," or a "bunch." The correct term is a *band.*

3. Timothy D. Pruitt, "Cricket Gangs," *Northeastern Nevada Historical Society Quarterly* 78-3 (Summer 1978): 115–16.

4. He was describing a *spermatophore.*

5. Pruitt, "Cricket Gangs," 115.

6. Darrel T. Gwinne, "Sexual Selection and Sexual Differences in Mormon Crickets (Orthoptera: Tettigoniidae, *Anabrus simplex*)," *Evolution* 38: 1011–22.

7. Ibid., 1013–18.

Chapter 23. Johanne

1. The history of the early life of Johanne Jorgensen given here is adapted from a eulogy delivered at her funeral. This narrative differs in minor details from other accounts of her early life. (Cyril Call, eulogy, November 1982, author's collection.)

Chapter 24. Lakeside

1. It was called a "platform," even though it was just a dirt path level with the tops of the ties.

2. This was Palmer's second year at Montello and Turner's first.

3. *National Youth Administration:* A government organization, established within the Works Progress Administration in 1935, that at first sought to obtain part-time work for unemployed youths and later shifted its emphasis to training them for war-related work.

4. When he registered to vote in October 1936, John Tofanelli indicated that he

had lived in Montello for twenty-four years but gave Italy as his place of birth. Was he christened Giovanni?

5. *Butterfly:* A slip of paper attached to a weight that could be thrown off a passing train where the section gang was working.

6. *Aligning bar:* A round steel bar four or five feet long with one end square and ending in a wedge-shaped point. Sometimes referred to as a *crowbar.*

7. To keep everyone together, one of the crew would call out a signal such as "Yo!" or "Heave!" or "Ahora!" How they determined who would do the calling was always a mystery to me. Somehow there was always someone who did it.

8. *Ballast:* The material—usually gravel, crushed rock, or slag—under and between the ties. Nearly all of the Western Pacific track in Nevada was ballasted with gravel, while the Southern Pacific used crushed rock. Crushed rock ballast was considered superior to gravel since it would give a little under the train wheels, thus providing a cushion and a smoother ride.

9. The head of a *tamping pick* had a sharp point on one end like a regular pick, but the other end terminated in a broad bit about two inches wide.

10. For safety reasons, it was a firm rule that when a crew was working on one set of a double track, all work ceased and both tracks were cleared when a train passed on either track.

11. *Gauge spiking:* On a standard-gauge railroad, when a new rail is set in place, it has to be positioned 56½ inches from the other rail. A track gauge is used to set the distance, and the rail is spiked in four or five places along its length before the rest of the spikes are driven.

12. A *spike maul* has a slender wooden handle attached to a narrow cylindrical head about fifteen inches long. The length of the head allows the spiker to drive a spike across the rail from where he is standing. The combination of thin handle and long head makes it necessary to keep the handle horizontal on impact to keep from breaking it.

Chapter 25. Elwood

1. Frank Elwood Call, "Autobiography," (author's collection, 1963), 1.

2. Willard C. Call, "Private Diary of Willard C. Call: Remembrances and Biographies." "A History of the Willard Call Family." 929.273, Film No. 1421912, Family History Library, Salt Lake City, 64.

3. F. E. Call, "Autobiography."

4. Ibid.

5. W. C. Call, "Diary," 68.

6. F. E. Call, "Autobiography."

7. W. C. Call, "Diary," 70.

8. F. E. Call, "Autobiography."

9. Ibid.

10. Ibid.

11. Ibid.

12. Ibid.

Chapter 26. Foreman

1. Marriages and families of the children of Frank E. and Johanne Call are as follows:

Frank Wendell Call married Delilah Rollins of Chicago, Illinois, and Lovell, Wyoming, August 30, 1943, in Billings, Montana. They had eleven children, one of whom died in an accident.

Rey Lucero Call married Arlene Johnson of Chicago, August 30, 1943, in Salt Lake City. They had eleven children, one of whom died in an accident.

Grant Aaron Call married Shirley Millie Jenson of Corinne, Utah, April 25, 1947, in Salt Lake City. They had seven children.

Dale El Call married Elda Louise Godfrey of Ogden, Utah, September 12, 1947, in Salt Lake City. They had five children.

Adona Call married Eugene Stephen Nye of Ogden, Utah, April 7, 1948, in Salt Lake City. They had ten children.

Cyril Call married Joanne Taylor of Ogden, Utah, June 1, 1951, in Salt Lake City. They had six children, one of whom died.

Lynn Bowen Call married Judy Davis of Perry, Utah, August 1, 1963, in Salt Lake City. They had six children, two of whom died.

As of this writing, the living posterity of Frank E. and Johanne Call numbers nearly three hundred, including spouses.

Bibliography

Adams, Ramon F. *The Language of the Railroader.* Norman: University of Oklahoma Press, 1977.

Annual Report of Beowawe School District, Eureka County, Nevada, for the Year Ending June 30, 1934. Nevada State Library and Archives, Carson City.

Call, Willard C. *Private Diary of Willard C. Call: Remembrances and Biographies.* "A History of the Willard Call Family." 929.273, Film No. 1421912, Family History Library, Salt Lake City.

Eureka (Nevada) Sentinel. Various issues, January–March 1932.

Gwinne, Darrel T. "Sexual Selection and Sexual Differences in Mormon Crickets (Orthoptera: Tettigoniidae, *Anabrus simplex*)." *Evolution* 38: 1011–22.

Hanft, Robert M. *Red River: Paul Bunyan's Own Lumber Company and Its Railroads.* Chico: California State University, 1980.

Morgan, Dale L. *The Humboldt: Highroad of the West.* New York: Rinehart, 1943.

Nevada State Senate. *Appendix to Journals of Senate and Assembly of the Thirty-Ninth Session of the Legislature of the State of Nevada, 1939,* Volume II: *State of Nevada Educational Directory and Information as to Certification of Teachers and Retirement Salaries,* November 1938.

Partridge's Dictionary of Slang and Unconventional English. New York: Macmillan, 1989.

Pruitt, Timothy D. "Cricket Gangs." *Northeastern Nevada Historical Society Quarterly* 78-3 (Summer 1978): 115–16.

Westcott, Lynn H. *Steam Locomotives.* Waukesha, Wisc.: Kalmbach, 1960.